AF328660

The Science
Behind
Digital
Transformations

INTELLIGENT CHANGE

ALEXANDER BUDZIER
THOMAS GOTTSCHALCK
KIM BJØRN THUESEN
ASTRID LANNG

WILEY

To Sarah, Anneliese, and our two cats, the latter of whom have the annoying habit of walking over the keyboard at precisely the wrong moment.
—Alexander

This book is the result of engaging discussions, hard work, and fun times. Thank you, Katrine, Alex, Frederik, Mads, Andreas, and Thomas for great times together. Also, this book is a reminder of how privileged we are to be part of a company that truly values deepening your understanding, widening your perspectives, and getting to work with what lights a fire in your eyes.
—Astrid and Kim

Contents

Acknowledgments

Writing a book is a challenging and rewarding endeavor, and we could not have done it without the support and encouragement of many people.

First and foremost, this was a group effort among dear friends. Our combined insight, expertise, and dedication were instrumental in shaping this book and bringing it to fruition. Our unwavering commitment to excellence and our contagious enthusiasm for the topic inspired us every step of the way.

We are particularly grateful to our families. We want to thank them for their love, patience, and understanding. They provided a nurturing environment and a sense of purpose that sustained us throughout this project.

We are indebted to our colleagues and collaborators, who generously shared their knowledge and resources with us. They challenged us to think deeply and critically about our ideas, helped us refine our arguments, and improved our writing. We are incredibly grateful to the hundreds of interviewees who generously gave their time to share insights and tell their stories. Their contributions were invaluable.

We also want to thank Andreas Leed, who assisted with our research. This book would not have been possible without his support and hard work. Frederik Jakob Madsen and Mads Lomholt were also integral to making the research happen through their invaluable efforts throughout the project.

Finally, we want to express our gratitude to you, the readers of this book. We hope that our book will inspire and inform you and enhance your understanding of how to lead digital transformations.

Introduction

Implementing new solutions, systems, and organizational processes is a significant challenge. In December 2005, Queensland awarded IBM a contract worth AUD 95 million (USD 72.2 million) to replace its aging payroll system.

Three years later, the project had yet to make much progress. IBM estimated it would take AUD 181 million (USD 154 million) to complete the project. The project was swiftly descoped to cover only the health sector for AUD 6.2 million (USD 5.3 million).[1]

In 2010, after 10 aborted go-lives and two and a half years behind the original deadline, the new system was finally operational at a cost of AUD 25.7 million (USD 23.6 million). However, the system did not work. It produced 35,000 payroll mistakes. At the peak of the errors, 1,010 employees were required to fix the data to make the fortnightly payroll run, at an annual cost of approximately AUD 170 million (USD 156.1 million).

An inquiry into the saga found many failings of governance, technical specifications, frequent scope changes, and a lack of project management capabilities.

Sometimes failure can follow even when the team gets the basics right. For example, the Danish University and Property Agency, known as Bygningsstyrelsen, designed a system that precisely met the specifications, met every deadline, and successfully delivered the requested product but failed to bring about the desired change within the organization.

After Bygningsstyrelsen went live with the new system, employees abandoned agreed-on work processes and instructions in favor of old, Excel-based methods during day-to-day operations. This failure to make changes caused all benefits of the digital transformation to disappear.

The problem in such situations typically is not technical; there is nothing wrong with the technology or system. The challenge lies with the people, politics, and cultures that must change to bring about the benefits.

Unfortunately, it does not matter how good new systems and processes are if nobody is willing to use them. Any technology endeavor that involves significant changes in people, power, and politics requires work to make those changes happen – not only in high-level strategies and ambitions but in manifested behavioral change at all levels of the organization.

Without investing effort into effective change management, the transformation risks failure – and most certainly will fail.

However, if change is managed successfully, it can help you secure the project's benefits on the first attempt.[2] By ensuring that the project meets the needs of both the organization and the people who will be using and be affected by the new systems, you can minimize the risk of wasting valuable resources on a failure.

The challenge here, however, is that managing organizational change requires a different skill set than managing a technical change. In this case, success requires people skills. Unfortunately, there is no technical solution to people skills; we have checked.

Another unfortunate fact is that there is very little scientific evidence on what digital transformation leaders do to make change management effective. A plethora of case studies and anecdotes exist, many of which suffer from survivor bias. Fortunately, we have been working hard to try to fix that problem.

How?

We know much about what digital transformations *should do* but little about what successful transformations *really do*. To build a systematic body of scientific data, we started a collaboration between the University of Oxford's Saïd Business School and Implement Consulting Group, based in Copenhagen.

At the University of Oxford, we were interested in better understanding the dynamics of organizational change and investments in information technology. Our previous research[3] shows that ineffective change management significantly contributes to cost overruns, schedule delays, and benefit shortfalls in digital transformations.

At Implement, we focus on ensuring that your efforts develop meaningful change within your organization by supporting you with implementing tools and techniques that have a meaningful impact. We help companies worldwide understand the human perspective and dynamics behind change.

Together, we desire to improve the success of digital transformations. We are basing this book on our combined 50+ years of experience working as consultants for businesses looking to implement change and our in-depth academic research into how to make sociotechnical change work.

We realized there was a lot of noise, confusion, and competing advice. So, we decided to systematically study existing research, to test, and to gather data on what worked and what did not.

We started by systematically reviewing the existing research and information on organizational and technological change, studying nearly 2,000 publications in the field. Based on this information and our combined knowledge, expertise, and insight, we identified the fundamental beliefs, opinions, and theories we wanted to examine and test in more detail.

We further validated and refined our approach and hypotheses through workshops with change experts. As a result, we identified seven "levers," or features, of digital transformations that might influence success.

Here are the seven levers of successful digital transformations:

1. *A clear reason to change* is the cornerstone of any successful transformation. It provides a vision, framework, and approach for digital transformations and sets the direction and purpose for the change.
2. *A defined approach to managing change* is the framework and precise plan for the digital transformation down to the last detail.
3. *Early involvement of users* in designing and testing processes and systems is necessary.
4. *Management ownership of the change* is the work of top, middle, and frontline management, not the project, to support, promote, and demonstrate ownership of the digital transformation.
5. *Effective communication* is not just a tool; it's a necessity for securing the commitment of stakeholders to the changes, and it is the transformation's active, deliberate dialogue that ensures everyone is on board with the digital transformation.
6. *Effective training* must equip users with the knowledge and practice of new working methods to ensure that users adopt new systems and processes.
7. *Establishing trust-based relationships* is not just a goal but a necessity. Digital transformations must create and maintain productive, trust-based relationships with end users and senior stakeholders.

We then carried out our research by analyzing 155 separate digital transformations. To be considered in our research, each transformation had to:

- Implement a technological component.
- Introduce organizational change, such as how employees use a system or their processes of work.
- Have completed the digital transformation for more than three months so we could evaluate its impact.

To gather our data, we interviewed those involved and analyzed data and statistics regarding how the transformation was managed and its long-term impact and effectiveness.

We then tested the seven levers to determine which ones are truly important.

We found that all seven levers contribute, directly or indirectly, to the long-term success of the transformation, though they have varying degrees of impact. These levers can be applied independently or jointly to calibrate your approach and ensure its success.

We discuss each of these levers separately throughout this book – their importance, examples of their applications in action, and common beliefs about them.

Chapters 1 and 2 the nature of change, how we carried out our research, and the value of effectively coordinating the change management aspect of a project implementation. Chapters 3 to 10 analyze the seven levers in more detail using case studies from our research to illustrate our findings.

The Purpose of This Book

In this book, we do not provide the perfect how-to recipe for digital transformation success. As you will soon discover, while our data show particular elements to be more effective than others, making a one-size-fits-all approach is a fool's errand.

Digital transformations align people's needs and wants with the organization's culture, needs, and wants. Because you will never find two situations in which these things neatly agree – and, most often, they are unknown at the outset – no easy recipe exists to resolve the people, power, and politics of change.

Instead, we analyzed the data we gathered and used case studies from our research, public information, and previous clients to explain how these levers impact and influence the success or failure of digital transformations.

This is not a should-do book but a what-works-and-why book. By reading it, you will learn the logic behind what digital transformations do, what works, and why. We hope you will discover new answers and inspirations that fit your needs.

Change Jargon Demystified

- *Digital* – We use the term "digital" to mean information technology (IT) and information systems (IS), the backbone of products, business processes, sales channels, and supply chains.[4]
- *Digital transformation* – We use the concept of transformation to emphasize the element of organizational change required to integrate and exploit investments in new digital technologies through changing organizational capabilities, business models, operational processes, and user experience.[5]

- *Project* – The temporary organization built to design, implement, and successfully deliver technological and organizational change. This organization has its team, resources, processes, systems, deadlines, and goals, and a strategy to deliver the changes. Once the organization has implemented the digital transformation, it typically dissolves, which makes it temporary. We know some companies are moving from projects toward a product-based approach to developing technology. We also see that transformations require dedicated projects once the changes impact multiple products, processes, and diverse groups of stakeholders and users.
- *Permanent organization* – The organization or company that owns the digital transformation.
- *End users* – The employees who work directly with the systems and processes about to change.
- *Stakeholders* – Our shorthand for senior stakeholders: senior managers and executives of the organization who have an interest or are instrumental in the change.
- *Communication specialist* – A professional working in communications who might be part of the transformation team or work for the permanent organization in a permanent organization, for example, in the communications department.
- *Change specialist* – An expert in organizational change and transformation management; in our case studies, variously an internal expert or often a consultant.
- *Steering committee* – A decision-making forum for the transformation's duration, typically bringing together the key senior stakeholders to provide governance in terms of setting targets, aligning transformation and business objectives, scrutinizing the transformation, and holding the transformation team accountable.
- *Manager (frontline/middle/top)* – A simplified view of the different hierarchical layers of management: Top management consists of the most senior executives involved in the transformation, frontline managers are the first layer of hierarchy above the end users, and middle management are the ones in between. We analyze this hierarchy in more detail in Chapter 7.
- *Technical change* – The activities focused primarily on changes to software, systems, products, services, and other assets; in some cases, technical change is even involved in the construction of new offices and the like.
- *Organizational change* – The activities to manage changes in employees' and customers' behavior, mindsets, attitudes, thinking, ways of working, and the like.

CHAPTER 1

What Does It Mean to Manage Digital Transformations?

No organization can avoid change forever – no matter how much it might want to. One of our favorite jokes about Oxford goes, "How many Oxford dons [professors] does it take to change a lightbulb?" The answer is: "Change? Change? CHANGE?!"

Continuing to use the same methods, technology, or approaches eventually means that you get left behind because you have failed to adapt to new realities or opportunities. Equally, however, you cannot embrace something simply because it is that new shiny thing that looks cool but does not offer your organization real value.

The allure of the shiny means that change needs to be rational – actively controlled and coordinated. This paradox of exploring and exploiting innovations, was first discussed by James G. March, a professor at Stanford University. He distinguished the two concepts by the degree of uncertainty of the returns for the organization. The returns of explorations are more uncertain than those of exploitations. But he argued that both are crucial for improving performance and competitive advantages.[1] The crucial insight is that every digital transformation must trade off exploration and exploitation. If the focus is solely on exploitation, the transformation misses an opportunity for innovation. If the focus is solely on exploration, the transformation misses the opportunity for relevant learning, changes, and results. All change should be happening with purpose.

Exploring and exploiting is not the only paradox of digital transformations. Organizations must also balance the conflicting and paradoxical demands of stability and change.[2] Counterintuitively, stable organizations are more effective at adopting change.[3]

In 2000, Jack Moran, a distinguished change practitioner in healthcare and adjunct professor at Arizona State University, and Baird Brightman, a clinical psychologist and writer about the human side of work, defined managing change as "the process of continually renewing an organization's direction, structure, and capabilities to serve the ever-changing needs of external and internal customers."[4]

Most people agree that change happens all the time. In the 1980s, leading thinkers on change and organizations identified another paradox between planned and unplanned changes.[5] Planned changes are responses to anticipated events. However, not all events can be anticipated, due to the turbulent environment in which organizations operate. Unplanned changes are responses to an unanticipated event that occur after the event happens.

These unplanned changes frequently lead to significant breakdowns, scandals, and organizational failure unless organizations retain an element of flexibility and fluidity to respond to unanticipated events through unplanned change.[6]

Rare events and crises also trigger organizational change. The argument goes that organizations in crisis failed to change before the crisis and are now scrambling for a response. Had they changed earlier, the crisis would not have happened. The underlying assumption in this argument is that all changes can be planned for. Our research finds that this is not true.[7] Thus, the ability to manage change is a crucial capability for every organization.[8]

But What Is This Managing Change?

According to Jerry Porras and Robert C. Silver from Stanford University, managing change involves:

- Using a set of theories, values, strategies, and techniques
- Aimed at the planned change of organizational vision and work settings
- To generate cognitive changes in members of the organization, manifesting in behavioral change and thus
- Promoting paradigmatic change that helps the organization better fit or create desirable future environments.[9]

In other words, managing change has become an area of special expertise that links strategic change to the daily tick-tock of operations. Change management is vital to ensure that organizations do not become victims of change but are change agents.

A more contemporary view makes a distinction between episodic and continuous change.[10] Looking at organizations from a macro perspective shows relatively stable ways of organizing work that is interrupted episodically to reconfigure the ways of working. At the same time, small changes happen constantly when the organization is viewed at the micro level. Indeed, the ability to manage small changes consistently is one of the critical characteristics of organizations that work reliably in uncertain environments.[11]

We are all familiar with the experience of small changes and innovations scaling to reach a tipping point. Consider, for example, the transformation that has, at some point, been nicknamed BYOD – Bring Your Own Device.

The turning point in the history of mobile phones was the release of the first iPhone in 2007. At that time, the BlackBerry dominated the market. The iPhone did not threaten the BlackBerry yet; the iPhone had a minimal battery life and a cumbersome keyboard, and, most of all, it wasn't secure. The core feature of the BlackBerry was security; it could securely operate email using servers that pushed new emails out to devices.

The idea of the BlackBerry was inspired by large companies that used systems like IBM's Lotus Notes, where email systems ran on mainframe-style solutions. This architecture was highly secure because it was tightly controlled. Back then, the IT department controlled access to servers, and users could get a BlackBerry only from the company's IT department.

The iPhone, however, improved and innovated on the BlackBerry; with a better camera and better internet browsing, it quickly became more attractive, and other devices followed suit. Suddenly, the consumer market offered innovation at a rate faster than the ability of IT departments to refresh their equipment.[12] In many organizations, the defined processes to manage technology change were not fast enough to meet end users' requirements for speed.

In some companies, Bring Your Own Device started because employees figured out how to forward emails to personal accounts or how to configure access to a mailbox from their phones.

What started as a small change by some tech-savvy individuals quickly grew – suddenly requiring a BYOD policy to keep emails secure. Macro changes were being triggered because of continuous micro changes. Many organizations needed to start a project to handle this digital transformation toward BYOD.

Our key observation is that change management is not a question of either/or; change is exploration and exploitation, unplanned and planned, episodic and continuous. Looking across different sectors, we find that the organizational challenge to change has increased in breadth and depth.

Organizations increasingly must collaborate internally to respond to current challenges, which require more depth, and with other organizations, which require more breadth. Again, few organizations find it easy to collaborate across internal silos, levels of hierarchy, and external boundaries with collaboration partners through existing processes and structures. The typical response is to start a project to deliver the transformation.

Not everyone benefits from change. Every change has its heroes, villains, and victims.[13] The core challenge for managing change is maximizing the positive impacts of changes on individuals and organizations while minimizing the negative impacts.

Therefore, change management is the set of management activities to plan, organize, staff, lead, control, and implement change so that it is effective, beneficial, and lasting. Often change management is seen as a specific task or project – such as building a house – with defined frameworks, practices, and processes. You can order change to happen, and it will do so successfully.

Unfortunately, change is not so simple in reality.

When an organization's leaders are planning and structuring digital transformations, they might believe they can task a change specialist to come in and restructure or transform how the organization operates and then leave. Once the specialist is gone, the change endures. We, however, know that this approach has not worked; it is said that 80% of digital transformation initiatives fail.[14]

Our research, which covers more than 6,000 IT projects, shows that if we evaluate projects by looking at how they delivered against the promises made in the investment decision:

- 59% of IT projects deliver on budget or better,
- 9% of IT projects deliver on budget and on time or better, and only
- 0.7% of IT projects deliver on budget, time, and benefits or better.

It is essential to recognize that the literal interpretation of the common term "change management" may not reflect the best approach. Managing change is not an administrative, stable, managerial activity. Experts in this field have started using more active words to replace "change management," such as "managing change," "changing work," or "transforming organizations."

Similarly, experts have stopped using the phrase "stakeholder management" because leaders engage with stakeholders rather than directly administer them. For this reason, we believe the industry needs to start viewing change management as a tool for leading transformations through others rather than simply administering changes.

We fundamentally believe that change cannot be directly managed and controlled. Data from our research, which we share in Chapters 3 to 10 of the book, have shifted our thinking.

Therefore, change management needs to address the central question and problem: How do we transform through technology successfully? Change also challenges core ideas about the organization – what it does, its purpose, and the identities of the people working for it. There are two sides to this:

1. Technology change involves identifying what the change should be – implementing a new technical or digital solution or changing products, processes, or how people operate – and rolling it out throughout the organization.
2. Organizational change involves working with the people affected by the technology change. For any change to succeed, it needs to be accepted and adopted by the people it affects. The journey toward transformation must ensure that the people involved in the change are not left behind. We need to support the people on this journey as best as possible.

However, to understand the importance of people in the context of significant technology change, we need to examine the origins of managing technology and organizational change and how people traditionally have perceived both.

History and Context of Managing Technological and Organizational Change

Awareness of the need to manage organizational changes in technology implementations started long ago. In our literature research, the oldest text we found on this topic was published in 1939 by Elliott Dunlap Smith, then professor of economics at Yale University.[15] Smith observed that successful transformations happened only when management (called "the capital" in the language of the 1930s) opened a dialogue and listened to their workers ("the labor") about the change.

Smith studied multiple cases in textile mills across the East Coast of the United States. All 18 mills he studied were hit hard by the Great Depression in the 1930s and needed to cut costs by 30% or more. The mills' mottos were uniformly: "Do more with less." Some mills succeeded and turned around, but the change failed spectacularly in many others.

In these cases, the solution was called the multiple-loom system – comprising repairing and replacing looms and frames – and a different, Taylorian, style of working, in which tasks shifted from skilled, high-paid weavers to unskilled labor, and weavers now operated many more looms.

The new multiple-loom system, combined technology improvements and new organizational practices to transform how the mills operated. However, in some mills workers were not involved in designing or implementing the change; these workers were expected to accept it quietly for the benefit of management. They did not. They sabotaged looms, spoiled goods, and organized walk-out strikes in protest; as a result, those mills went bankrupt.

Smith's research showed us that labor and technology must be managed together – you cannot simply drop a technology on a large organization and hope it works. Without ensuring that the people affected by a change understand and accept the new technology, you cannot expect them to use it happily and effectively.

For leaders of technology transformations, Smith had these words of advice:

> Like marriage, the effort to [transform] . . . even if this [change] is good, is something to be entered into "soberly, reverently, and in fear of God," and, I may add, with sufficient financial resources to see through much more expenditure than is superficially apparent.[16]

The turning point at which change management got put on the map, however, was in 1995, thanks to the work of John Kotter, professor at Harvard and the best-known author on change. Kotter created a top-down, eight-step model informed by many failed initiatives for change. He suggested the eight factors that typically lead to failure and the eight steps to take to avoid them.[17]

1. Establishing a sense of urgency
2. Forming a powerful guiding coalition
3. Creating a vision
4. Communicating the vision
5. Empowering others to act on the vision
6. Planning for and creating short-term wins
7. Consolidating improvements and producing still more change
8. Institutionalizing new approaches

The eight steps outline a neat process that starts at the organization's top, creating a sense of urgency – often around declaring a crisis or a burning platform. Senior leaders with authority set up a steering committee: the guiding coalition. A vision then needs to be created and communicated.

Leaders empower others to make small changes by declaring a big change. They often use consultants to bypass resistant managers. These changes are celebrated and institutionalized through new policies and standard operating procedures.

While, arguably, knowing the causes for failure does not necessarily mean that avoiding these causes guarantees success, Kotter's work brought change management into the public eye. Since 1995, when Kotter's article first appeared, our understanding of change has moved on dramatically.

Kotter's insights suggested a process we frequently see being applied in practice. First, you define your vision and objectives and then mobilize employees to create the change. However, Kotter's model does not explicitly advise defining the solution at the top and rolling it out top down. But all too often, when organizational change is combined with technology change, both the delivery of new technology and the organizational change follow a top-down waterfall approach, an approach that often is inflexible.

Today, other approaches to organizing change, such as lean and agile, offer different perspectives. Their focus is on flexibility of the solution, speed, and innovation.

Since Kotter's article was published, business leaders' awareness of the value of change management has grown.

Researching successful change has increased; previously, change was not considered a field of study. Now researchers devote time and resources to understand change better. Citation databases, such as Scopus and Web of Science, which track the creation and citation of written materials on specific subjects, are practical tools for measuring this development. Figure 1.1 shows the explosion in publications on change management since 1995.

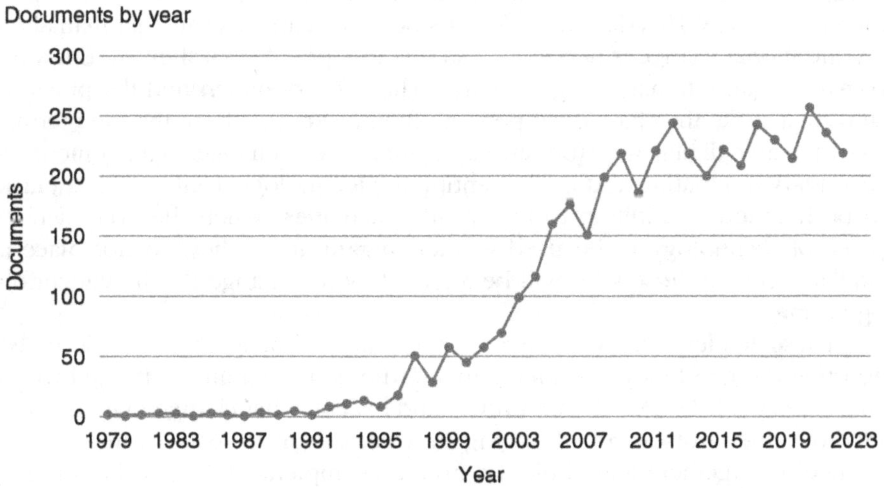

FIGURE 1.1 Annual volume of academic publications on change management.

A second tipping point happened in the technology community. In February 2001, 17 software developers penned the Agile Manifesto.[18] The idea of greater agility – more responsive, flexible, iterative approaches to implementing technologies – was not new, but the manifesto started a revolution.

Today, agile projects are firmly established as practical approaches to implementing digital transformations. Throughout the book, we discuss the value and impact of the agile approach.

Challenges in Managing Change

In our experience, leaders recognize and accept the need to manage change and know the pitfalls. Our results show that two-thirds of leaders have a structured or defined approach to change. (See Chapter 5 and Appendix B for details.) However, often there are considerable differences in the perceptions of what change approaches entail.

Frequently leaders fail to account for imperfect strategies and imperfect strategy implementation – the inability to adjust for your people and their needs. Some people still vividly believe that change can be controlled – that taking actions A and B always leads to result C. Therefore, once they have planned how to change people and delivered on each step, they expect the result to match their planned and predicted outcome.

While leaders recognize the value of managing change, there is a significant disconnect between realizing the need for it and successfully implementing change. This disconnect occurs because leaders know that managing organizational change is necessary and involves people, but they are unaware of what organizational change requires. They do not understand the practical steps that make the change happen and then make it stick for the long term.

In many digital transformations, leaders view change management as secondary to creating and implementing the technology itself – an extra task to be handled in addition to the primary activities. When they buy a new piece of technology to be used in their organization, they do not place a similar focus on those who will be affected by the change this new technology brings.

These leaders might be aware that change management needs to be accounted for, but they consider it an afterthought. After all, everyone loves a shiny new tool. As they do not understand exactly what change management involves, they outsource – bringing in a consultant to lead a three-person change management team bolted onto the IT implementation without being properly integrated into the transformation.

On top of this, these leaders approach the role from a technical point of view and come up with lots of theories and anecdotal evidence that they are keen to put into practice.

This technical, rational, Newtonian approach to change management does not work to solve people-based issues with change, which, as we explain in this book, is one of the most critical factors to success. Organizational and people-based change both need to be integral parts of your thinking toward digital technologies. Without prioritizing both the organizational and the technological change equally, your organization's transformation is unlikely to be successful.

Case Study: Failure to Communicate

[Tom] A global logistics company started working on a huge transformation by implementing an enterprise resource planning (ERP) solution a year ago. To support the project, the company brought in a change team and have, to date, spent €5 million on the change management effort, which shows the scale and importance of this particular solution.

Due to a communications failure, however, the company is currently in huge trouble.

Leaders are implementing this new solution at a critical strategic location for the global logistics supply chain. However, only recently did the project manager learn that, despite a year having passed, there has yet to be any communication with the business unit running the strategic location in the supply chain. They had not heard anything about the transformation, nor had there been any dialogue about it.

While leaders had started well by hiring a change team, they had not prioritized paying attention to what was happening. They had assumed that having a change team would automatically make change happen.

This situation is a common one in digital transformations – awareness that organizational change is necessary on an intellectual level but failing to translate that awareness into successful implementation.

Flexible Support and Approach

When you are aware that a process is necessary but do not know how to do it, the logical response is to look for a manual. Project leaders, or whoever is in charge of directing the transformation, need to come up with the best supporting elements for the change that is happening. These elements include both tools and activities, such as dialogue with end users and stakeholders.

Thus, project leaders look for a specific recipe. They focus on organizational change as a technical problem to be solved, using tools and activities that might have worked for others but neglecting to account for the cultural aspect and people.

The lack of a recipe is often deeply frustrating to leaders – they followed every step correctly, but the transformation still did not work. The trouble is that they did not understand the purpose and weight behind the steps and were applying approaches that were not right for their situation.

… Until It Feels Right

[Kim] Learning recipes is not an effective way to learn how to cook. It is far more effective to know when and how to use techniques. I experienced this when I started learning how to bake bread for myself.

I had bought a recipe book from a renowned expert in Denmark. I expected that because the person writing it knew their stuff, I would be an expert myself in no time. However, I found the instructions vague. I had to deal with instructions like "Knead the bread until it feels right."

All I had wanted was a simple recipe to make bread! I was no baker and did not understand what "feels right" was meant to feel like. I might have understood intellectually why I had to knead the bread, but the recipe offered me no support with the practical side.

To make things more complicated, little things – such as using the same type of flour but from different brands – made it so that I could not rely on simplifying my approach to "knead for 4 minutes exactly."

I understood the instructions only after learning what "right" felt like and how to adapt my approach to different ingredients. These days, I can use the book easily.

[Alex] You might wonder what Kim's learning has to do with digital transformations. The same journey plays out in expert learning. The brothers Stuart and Hubert Dreyfus – one an applied mathematics professor and one a philosopher of artificial intelligence – developed a model that has become fundamental in explaining why experts feel what's "right."[19] Their model of learning starts with the novice stage. Whether you are a novice in baking bread or driving transformations, you begin by learning the recipes.

We all start by achieving a task through learning a series of steps:

- Follow the recipe.
- Decompose problems into components.
- Tackle each problem in turn.
- Make analytical decisions.
- Monitor the outcomes.

When tasked with driving a transformation, *novices* also have a recipe to follow. When faced with specific tasks, problems, or challenges, they have process models and frameworks they can apply. For example:

- To engage with stakeholders, use a template to map and develop an engagement plan.
- To make decisions about a problem, conduct analyses, and use rational techniques like analytical hierarchical decision making.
- To measure the success of endeavors, define performance indicators.

At the next stage of learning, *advanced beginners* start exploring what rules apply given a particular context – which shortcuts can be taken and which are better avoided. At this stage, we develop situational knowledge that guides us in tailoring our approach.

Competent experts recognize more complex patterns and the interrelations between adjacent challenges in the transformation – for example, the links among stakeholder engagement, communication strategy, and building the commitment to change.

Proficient experts then make decisions predominantly based on intuition – positive heuristics, as Gerd Gigerenzer, director of the Max Planck Institute for Human Development, calls these intuitions.[20] Transformation leaders have a few rules of thumb to organize the transformation activities. When we interviewed transformation leaders, the number 1 heuristic, for example, was "Get Your Team Right."[21] Up to this point, experts had used guiding principles, and now they intuit their course of action.

Finally, true experts or *masters of a field* develop a radar for how things are going. Their intuition applies not only to decisions but also to their awareness of outcomes. Masters in their field notice weak signals of whether a transformation is going well. They absorb themselves in a situation and develop ideas about what must be done.

For example, their radar for the energy levels of the project team might tell them that setbacks have arisen that team members may not have recognized yet. For this reason, masters may begin challenging the team's assumptions.

As we all develop our expertise in driving transformations, we move from (see Figure 1.2):

- Follow the recipe → Use adaptable approaches
- Decompose problems into components → Study the problem context

- Tackle each problem in turn → Solve interconnected challenges
- Make analytical decisions → Intuitive decision making
- Monitor the outcomes → Absorbing weak signals

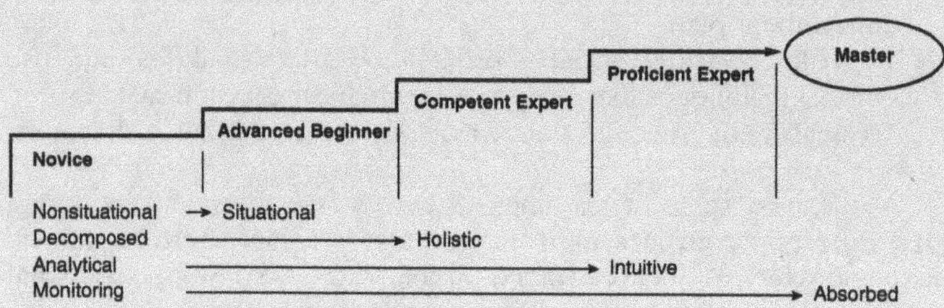

FIGURE 1.2 The Dreyfus and Dreyfus model of learning.
Source: Adapted from Stuart E. Dreyfus and Hubert L. Dreyfus. 1986. *Mind over Machine.* Free Press.

The first key takeaway from understanding how novices become masters is to recognize that we all learn from trial and error. As in Kim's baking lesson, you can have all the right ingredients for managing change, combine them according to the recipe, and still get the wrong result.

As in baking bread, the real sign of skill in managing change comes in the "kneading" and the "proving" – knowing instinctively in which situation you require more kneading and less proving. Once you have developed the intuition to correctly meet the problem at hand without needing to second-guess yourself – giving your bread the right time to rise without wasting time measuring the temperature and calculating manually – you have mastered the necessary skills.

The second key takeaway is how we teach others to master change. A novice on our team needs a recipe. Leaders need to give novices a recipe with steps to follow, allow them to make mistakes, and coach them to learn from their mistakes.

In digital transformations, you need to develop your skills so that you can avoid ending up with a severely over- or under-baked IT project.

It would be best to consider implementing digital transformations less of a rigid recipe and more about adapting and reacting to the specific needs of the people and organization. For this reason, engaging with the people the change is affecting is so important – with an open dialogue, you can work together to find the approach that feels right.

Another example is raising children. You cannot raise two different children in the same way – even if you teach them precisely the same lessons, read them the same books, and provide the same dinners, they will learn different things and grow into different people.

Part of parenting is tailoring your approach to fit what your child needs or wants, without unthinkingly assuming that your quiet, shy bookworm will automatically love playing full-contact rugby as much as their wilder and more energetic sibling.

Similarly, you cannot treat all organizations – or the individuals in them – the same way and expect them to behave or adjust to new systems, methods, and processes the way you wish. Because we are unable to predict how each organization might react, we must tailor support to fit as required. Doing this requires a flexible approach and a toolbox for change management that understands how to change behavior or educate behavior as needed.

Unfortunately, business leaders who can bridge the gap between intellectually understanding the need and successfully acting on it are usually only those who have been burned once or twice. They learn to take implementing organizational change seriously – rather than seeing it as secondary to the technology change – only after they have been put in situations where doing the assumed right thing turned out badly.

The point of this book is to ensure that you do not need to suffer from this frustration.

What Are Our Goals Here?

When approaching digital transformations, there are many possible causes for frustration and confusion. While it is clear that managing change is essential, executing it is hard. The sheer amount and diversity of suggested strategies are bewildering. In our daily work and research, we have found more than 240 different frameworks to choose from.

Even when you have a framework and a strategy, it is too easy to suffer the frustration of following your strategy perfectly but still failing. The experience required to succeed often comes at the cost of previous failures.

Our aim in writing this book is to relieve some of the frustration, stress, and confusion associated with managing change. In the next chapter, we trace the origins of the first principles. Before we take a close and critical look at which principles benefit you and which might be more important than others.

We explore how you move forward from these first principles – looking at how others have integrated them to drive transformational change and how you can do the same.

This greater understanding of digital transformations will unlock opportunities for you. You can look at your current projects from a fresh perspective – seeing how to improve and make these projects deliver their intended outcomes. You can approach future projects differently by thinking more clearly about how to set up the transformation from the start.

Unfortunately – or perhaps fortunately – we do not offer a one-size-fits-all framework or recipe for digital transformations that will work for everyone. Instead of trying to do that, we demystify what managing change is for you by explaining what digital transformations do. Once you understand what digital transformations involve – and why they are essential – you can manage and implement your strategies far more effectively.

We hope that, by understanding how things work and why, you will avoid mistakes. Trying and failing *is* an effective way to learn how to find the approach that feels right. However, failing a digital transformation can be expensive and dangerous.

The consequences of misjudging what feels right are far steeper for leaders of organizational and technological change than for home bakers. For this reason, we want to help you understand what guides effective change management so you do not need to learn what it entails the hard way.

Who Are We? Why Do We Matter?

We were in the same position as many of our readers when we began working on this research. We knew that change management was critical, but we also knew the frustration, stress, and confusion we experienced when working on our digital transformations.

However, when we discovered more about change management, we were overwhelmed by the volume of information and noise on the subject. So, we sat down and began to analyze the existing knowledge systematically. Using our collective practical experience and expertise, we were able to make sense of what works and what does not work, sorting through confusing and sometimes conflicting evidence.

We distilled nearly 2,000 articles, books, conference papers, and similar texts into our first principles for successful digital transformations. Then, over hundreds of hours, we held a series of workshops with about 200 change practitioners, who brought their rich experiences to identify and validate the core principles that we all believe are important for successful digital transformations.

Our final task was to test those principles. Over three years, we looked for leaders involved in big digital transformations. We went through the University of Oxford alums and Implement Consulting Group client networks. We also created a list of big digital transformations we knew were underway.

In the end, we carried out an in-depth analysis of 155 digital transformations – interviewing those in charge of the project to deliver the transformation to build a collection of over 500 hours of interviews. In these interviews, we asked closed and open questions to get insights from graded scales that allow for comparison between different projects and recorded answers to the open follow-up questions, which allowed us to analyze each case in detail.

Then we asked for supporting evidence, including board presentations, investment proposals, project plans, cost reports, and project schedules, to obtain objective measures on cost overruns, schedule delays, and benefit shortfalls. The results of the analysis are discussed in Chapters 3 to 10 the book, and statistical analysis is presented in Appendix B.

We created this extensive data set to examine what happened in each transformation and how the core principles we had identified were used and to conduct rigorous statistical analysis of those principles to determine which ones were helpful.

Therefore, this book's conclusions, insights, and principles are entirely based on data-driven research. We also heard inspirational stories of transformations, which we share – as far as we can without breaking confidentiality – and describe novel ideas and approaches we have encountered.

Surprisingly, what we thought was true turned out not to be true. Using our research, we also reflected on our own experiences, and we were able to make sense of the setbacks we encountered, which we are happy to share. Through all of this, we discovered terrific new ideas. We learned from the frustration of others to spare you the same experience, so you can not only avoid some pitfalls but also make your challenging transformation more successful and fun.

We have taken what we have learned and applied this to other transformations. So far, we have seen marked improvements and successes – but then again, learning and innovation never stop. Read on to learn more about what we have discovered and how it might help you.

CHAPTER 2

The Business Case for Change Management

As discussed in Chapter 1, managing change is often a mysterious black box rife with jargon and countless frameworks. Business leaders know they should have someone manage change, but they need to understand it better and learn how to implement it effectively. Moreover, they underestimate and undervalue vital factors for success.

The most significant factor is motivating people to accept and adopt the change; if nobody is willing to use the technology, then the investment of introducing it is wasted. Sometimes, we illustrate this idea by using our very unscientific success formula.

Of course, we need a first-rate system with high data quality, usability, responsiveness, correctness, availability, and so on. We also need users to use the system.

In some cases, we have found ourselves in situations where change management was undervalued. Sometimes strange situations occur in which personnel are brought in specifically to manage change, but the activities they should coordinate never happen or approaches to facilitating the project are dismissed from the start. Watching such car crashes that could have been prevented if you had been listened to is the hardest part of the job.

So, to get everyone on the same page: Why is managing change necessary, and why is it essential to put in the effort to understand it and get it right?

A 2024 survey by Gartner, a market intelligence firm, asked chief executives about the top three priorities for their organization. Technology was priority number 2, after growth. Ninety-five percent of CEOs reported a digital transformation is underway in their organizations. On average, they spent 5% of their revenues on digital transformations but only 66% of the investment was useful; 34% was wasted.[3]

$$\text{Success} = \text{System quality} \cdot \text{Adoption}^2$$

Our formula is a simplified version of the seminal information system success model developed by Professors William H. DeLone and Ephraim R. McLean[1] and the recent research in this space.[2]

Our formula states that the success of any technology project rests on two things:

1. The quality of the system developed – which typically comprises data quality, system quality, and service or process quality
2. Most important, whether users adopt and use the system. System adoption is driven by several factors: user satisfaction, top management and line management support and control, user training, and intention to drive system adoption.

Ultimately, no matter how high quality your solution might be, you still need to work on acceptance; even the best system in the world can't function without users. The need to drive system acceptance and adoption makes change management as important part of a project as the solution design and build, since successful change management drives adoption.

Before 2010, organizations underwent significant changes only once a decade. Every decade or so, organizations would implement a massive project to integrate a technology that would be used for the next 10 – 20 years. IT investments were treated like industrial projects, like investments in building factories.

The scale of the projects justified any expenses – the investment could be written off slowly over the technology's long life span – and the benefits of modernization were usually clear, even if the business case broke even only after six or seven years.

This cycle has accelerated in recent years. Innovations are happening more regularly, and smaller-scale solutions are being offered. In *How Google Works*,[4] former Google CEO Eric Schmidt describes the modern process as "create a product, ship it, see how it does, design and implement improvements, and push it back out. Ship and iterate. The companies that are the fastest at this process will win."

In short, the faster companies play the game, the more they will dominate the market. Slow and steady no longer wins the race.

The increasing pace means that change needs to happen more often than once a decade – and getting the implementation right without wasting investment is more critical than ever.

The need to embrace modern technology and digitize your organization are now considered inevitable. Many leaders seem to think there is no option but to get on board. But digitizing organizations and introducing new technologies, like AI, can lead to problems; questions like "How is this beneficial to us?" or "Are we prepared for this?" are ignored. Going through changes without asking important questions risks failure and damage to the organization.

The speed of the changes required put organizations under pressure. To stay competitive, changes need to be made quickly. A detailed strategy to implement the technology is made, and money is invested. However, the human side of the implementation is often lost in the rush.

Technological changes are usually beneficial to the organization, at least on paper.[5] The weak link is often with the humans using this new technology. Learning to adapt to a new system is difficult, particularly when someone believes the previous one already met their needs. If it is hard for end users to see the new technology's benefits, they will revert to their old methods[6] or drag their heels through the roll-out period.

Technology change is essential, but a crucial part of change management is ensuring that the change is happening for a reason, not innovation for its own sake or to seem competitive, modern, and trendy. A solid strategy for managing change must stay aware of how it benefits the organization. Without focusing on securing and maintaining user adoption, even the most sensible project will turn into a white elephant.

Case Study: 13 Weeks to Fail

We came across a great idea in one bank we studied for our research.

Financial disruptors, such as new services or products invented by small-scale new players and competitors, pressured the bank. The bank's leaders knew that technology enabled their success, and they frequently had brilliant ideas for implementing a specific new technology that looked appealing. However, more is needed than unthinkingly implementing something just because it is new and exciting.

To bring some order to the chaos that ensued, the bank set up a special team called "13 Weeks to Fail." The idea was to try new technologies and make them fail faster and more cheaply.

(continued)

> *(continued)*
>
> If someone has a brilliant idea, the team starts working for 13 weeks to determine if the technology has a use case, works in compliance with regulations, and ticks the boxes for cybersecurity. Having done that, the team establishes how much time, money, and effort it would take to implement the technology. And, most important, the team identifies the benefits.
>
> After the 13 weeks passed, the team makes its recommendations: This should either turn into a proper project or be abandoned. As the team leader said, "The hardest thing for the team to learn was to say no to senior leaders. But we are getting increasingly better at it, and we are saying no increasingly often."

Banks and financial institutions often need to implement changes to stay competitive; new cybersecurity measures and innovations or compliance with new regulations are typical examples. Without these changes, the banks would go under. However, skilled project managers always look beyond necessity for the benefit and advantage.

Being able to provide strategic advantage is more motivating than simply saying "We must do this to survive." That mentality is akin to writing a blank check. Therefore, an organization like a bank needs to be aware of how improved cybersecurity benefits the people working there once the project has succeeded or how compliance with new regulations is a positive force.

As a project leader in a bank told us:

Whenever my team came to me with a new regulatory requirement, I asked how to turn it into a business requirement. Where a requirement was in an area of very stable and settled regulation, we overinvested to reduce future operations costs to the absolute minimum – that would give the bank a competitive advantage.

We also found requirements in areas where regulation was likely to shift and evolve. We went cheap and cheerful there and accepted many manual workarounds. Saving on capital investment gave us a competitive advantage in those instances.

By defining exactly what successful change will look like in the organization, ideally in an objectively measurable way, you can analyze how successful the transformation has been. Without a result that objectively benefits the organization and its people, you must question whether the change is worth the cost and disruption.

The Good, the Bad, and the Ugly

The worst form of change management is when there is none – the equivalent of the textile mills that introduced the new loom technology and new job roles and processes just by posting notices in the canteen.

As we have said, lousy change management occurs when lots of warm words and good intentions are put into a detailed strategy that fails to translate into actions. Too many change management frameworks put too much emphasis on analyzing and planning the change and too little on changing.

This approach results in the investment of time and money in planning and strategizing with no resulting rewards. Needs analyses might be completed, workshops attended, and people interviewed, but the project fails to lift the strategy off the PowerPoint pages. In our experience and based on our data, for every dollar spent planning IT projects, 10 dollars must be spent making the technological and organizational changes happen.

Overplanning and underaction are some of the many patterns of lousy change management. Another too-common pattern is when change management turns ugly. Kotter and Schlesinger[7] outlined six commonly used strategic approaches to managing change:

1. Education and communication
2. Participation and involvement
3. Facilitation and support
4. Negotiation and agreement
5. Manipulation and co-optation
6. Explicit and implicit coercion

Far too often, organizations race to the bottom of this ladder. They start with great intentions to persuade employees about the benefits of changes, and once they discover the amount of effort and work required, they co-opt and coax the changes. The rollout bulldozes into an organization like a bull in a china shop.

Often leaders justify using their authority to bulldoze change by declaring that in a crisis or an emergency, speed matters. So they say. In these situations, because timelines are fixed and the scope is fixed, there is very little flexibility and room to maneuver.

Case Study: Leadership in a Crisis

Common thinking is that a time-critical change project requires command and control. However, we learned that command and control is not actually the best approach when dealing with a crisis. Good change management principles equally apply.

As one of our interviewees told us:

One of my crisis projects was a situation we had with some software that was critical to the business. It was a system that we used to handle all contacts coming into our contact center through every single media channel. So, it would be collating everything that came in through Twitter and Instagram, people using the phone, and letters coming in, which would all go into this single system.

It wasn't a system we'd planned to touch—it was there, operational, and working—so it wasn't really on my radar [as the chief information officer] from a project's viewpoint until there was an issue with the supplier software. We had to respond quickly and move on to new software.

We scoped it out and ended up with a very, very simple objective: to get everything off this now-legacy platform and have something working on a new platform in less than 48 hours. So that was our challenge. It met the criteria of a crisis or emergency. It wasn't anything that had been planned for; it had a very, very fixed deadline that we had to meet.

The scope was crystal clear and essentially immovable, and we couldn't have left stuff where it was because where it was wasn't going to exist anymore, which left us with very limited levers to pull.

Our interviewee continued to reflect on his role as the leader of this crisis project. But his key takeaway was that an authoritative, command-and-control approach would overwhelm him. Instead, he explained his crucial insight in this way:

Leadership comes into its own on these kinds of blitz projects. There needs to be very, very strong leadership. You need to find a team to rally and rally them. You need to get everybody on the same page and buy into the same vision very, very quickly.

> *Throughout, you need to be the person who inspires, injects energy, and brings enthusiasm, energy, and passion. What I would advise anyone to do if they find themselves in this situation is make that mental separation. If you are leading this blitz project, you are a leader; you need to separate that from your management skills.*
>
> *If you still need the management elements, find somebody who can act as a manager for you to manage the processes to track delivery. By delegating the process management and reporting, you have time to focus on leadership, bringing your team together, letting them make the decisions, inspiring and rallying everyone toward a common goal.*

Good change management must be flexible and adaptable, in regular projects and even in times of crisis. Rather than taking an inflexible top-down approach that fails to adapt to or account for new developments or information, you need to act on new information. With good change management practices in place, success rates and stakeholder satisfaction are higher than in bad and ugly change management cases.

How Do We Know If It Works?

One of the most potent questions about any management advice is how you know it works. Based on our systematic literature review and our workshops with practitioner experts in the field, we concluded that there are three perspectives from which you can analyze and measure the success of digital transformations:

1. The project management perspective
2. The people involved
3. Benefits and results

Project Management Perspective

The most enduring measure of success in project management is the iron triangle: time, cost, and quality. To this date, Roger Atkinson's original article[8] is one of the most cited papers in the history of project management research.

We built on the iron triangle and what we learned from the project management literature to formulate that one perspective of transformation success is to deliver within budget, on time, and to the expected hard, measurable benefits. We deliberately replaced the quality leg of the iron triangle with benefits to integrate the three variables that go into calculating the net present value in the final investment decision.

The project manager's role is to ask if delivery against targets is happening. For the project to be successful, all three perspectives need to be true. There is no point in successfully delivering on time and within budget if the solution does not offer the desired benefit.

People

Good digital transformation management also involves being aware of how people feel about the project. For a project to succeed from a people perspective, the question is: Would the people in the organization, particularly those impacted by the change, do it again?

It is entirely possible for a project to be successful in other senses – it achieves the required change, benefits the organization, and is a more efficient solution that cuts costs – but nobody would repeat the project. In such cases, project managers have failed to look after the people who might have been pushed to work overtime while experiencing immense stress as the work climate becomes increasingly adversarial and toxic.

Thus, we examined the satisfaction of the project sponsor, frontline management, end users, and the project management team. Were they satisfied with the project? Did they think it was a success?

Case Study: Danish Tax Authority

The Danish tax authority is an example of the cost of mismanaging people in change initiatives. As a public institution, it is not going out of business; however, a symptom of its struggle is that it can be constantly restructuring.

This fact leads to a constant cycle of major organizational transformations. A center or system will be closed down because it is malfunctioning or costs too much. New implementation centers will be opened to handle the function instead, only to run into similar issues a few years later. The cycle of organizational restructuring starts again, with the new centers closing and their activities moving elsewhere.

The strategies and initiatives may have been sound; however, the tax authority's approach to its employees was lacking. Indeed, supposedly 40% of workers leave the organization.[9] This situation means that something went very wrong, and changes were not being delivered to the employees working there.

Benefits and Results

As we argued earlier, projects are measured by concrete metrics – whether they deliver on time and stay within budget, for example.

However, in most projects, these metrics are not targets; they are constraints. Our data clearly show that staying within project constraints indicates project management success rather than transformation success.[10] We must consider subjective measures to understand the transformation's success.[11]

What defines project success are not only the inputs and outputs and the cashable benefits but also the qualitative factors that characterize the outcomes. The organization's capabilities might grow, allowing it to achieve more in other contexts or projects, or better work practices like collaboration or knowledge exchange might become possible.

In addition to the inputs, outputs, and outcomes, you can consider the broader strategic contribution. What legacy has the project enabled? Does it allow future innovations? What lessons can be learned that will help the organization grow? Has working on the transformation team advanced the careers of the people involved?

Douglas Hubbard,[12] a management consultant and author in decision sciences, observed in his research and practical work that many organizations use performance measures with meager information value for decision making and do not use high-information-value measures. He termed this phenomenon "the measurement inversion." The antidote is to start thinking about the end goal and look farther than the easily measurable inputs, outputs, and outcomes.[13]

In our research, we investigated the qualitative benefits and results of digital transformations by asking:

- Did the project meet the expectations that were built among end users?
- Did the project deliver the promises it made?
- Did end users adopt the system as expected?
- Overall, did the project achieve the intended change impact?

Sadly, we often see that putting hours into measurable results and acting on the data afterward is too much work for some organizations. Sometimes the more qualitative benefits and results are ignored because they are difficult to measure or are unlikely to produce good news about the transformation.[14] Instead, some organizations prefer to unquestioningly trust that everything works and that the implementation succeeded before it even started.

Case Study: Failure

We've seen this hiding of failures before with a massive high-tech company's transformation of a core IT system.

This company is a telecommunications firm that provides a range of services, including mobile and fixed-line phones and internet access, to consumers and businesses. Unfortunately, the company's implementation failed so badly that it had to abandon the entire project.

The software was working, yet the business requirements had changed and shifted, making the system obsolete before it even went live; however, the company couldn't admit to having abandoned it. No one wanted to admit that they had thrown away the money that had been invested.

Therefore, it became some poor soul's duty to waste workdays in front of a useless computer system to validate that the system was still in use.

If the project ultimately fails, the human aspect is often ignored, and the technology itself is blamed for "not being user-friendly" or "being too complicated." Although these may be factors, and it is possible to choose the wrong tech entirely, the majority of transformations fail because the people within an organization fail to embrace it.

When major projects fail so spectacularly and waste all the money invested without creating any benefit, the failure typically is not one of technology. Even if the technology has flaws, they typically can and will be fixed. Projects often start because of a problem that requires a technological solution, but in the end, transformation success or failure always depends on humans. Even when projects encounter technical issues, they get abandoned only if the stakeholders lose patience and confidence.[15]

Other human reasons for the failure of a digital transformation might have been that end users were not ready to use the system, that they lacked training, or that stakeholders' strategies and priorities had shifted, eliminating the reason for putting the project into practical use. In other projects, the issue might lie with the humans delivering the transformation; a delivery strategy may have been too inflexible to adapt to a changing environment.

Or perhaps the system designed and implemented does not help end users solve the problem being addressed, which means there was likely poor communication from the start that prevented the solution from aligning with stakeholders' business objectives and needs.

This chapter started by asking what the business case for change management in digital transformation is. The insights are stark and clear. Without managing the organizational – the people – side of digital transformation, we are guaranteeing failure.

The logical next question is: What does managing organizational change entail to make digital transformations a success?

That is the topic of the remainder of the book, where we investigate the seven levers in detail.

CHAPTER 3

Seven Levers for Implementing Successful Change Management

Digital transformations face a double challenge. On the one hand, they need to deliver a high-quality technology solution, and on the other hand, they need to deliver lasting organizational change.

The field of change management is rife with frameworks for implementing transformations successfully. As mentioned earlier, our research collected more than 240 of these frameworks. Our primary focus in this research is on digital and technology transformations. These range from transformations – where the primary focus was to completely digitize a company – to cultural change, which nearly always has a digital aspect these days. Despite the enormous number of frameworks and guidance, there is not much data or research into precisely which factors impact the success of a transformation.

Our case studies and specific examples that we share and discuss inevitably focus on digital implementations and technology projects. Don't let that dissuade you from reading if the changes you are concerned about are not centered on technology. We provide relevant insights for all types of transformations.

As we carried out our research – which involved reading over 2,000 academic articles and conducting workshops with more than 200 experts, such as change managers and project managers who work with organizations implementing digital transformations – we identified seven key factors, or "levers," with which change can be managed.

These seven levers might not surprise anyone familiar with technology development and transformations; however, we identified common beliefs or misconceptions that we wanted to study and challenge. Too frequently, the experts developing frameworks fail to ask: "But how do we know it's working?" Often we do not challenge whether a novel idea, a single case study, or some lessons learned can scale and what advice is genuinely needed in what context.

Our goal here is to share our findings and data in a more engaging way. While academic papers are full of valuable information and insights, they are often focused on narrow aspects of change, and sometimes they are hard to fit into the complex puzzle that is transformation and transfer into practice.

The aim of this book is to understand the *why* and *how* of change based on rigorous academic research and to bring the findings to life with practical examples to show how change can be done.

In the next seven chapters, we examine the seven levers for change we have identified. As we review and explain our findings and conclusions, we also illustrate the rewards of successfully navigating the challenges – and the consequences of having overlooked or mismanaged them – using case studies from our research.

Each of the seven levers we have identified offers value and benefit to any transformation; some might directly impact the result, while others might provide more indirect benefits. While it is entirely possible to approach a transformation by focusing on only one or two of these levers, the more of them you actively consider in your planning and implementation, the better the transformation's chances of success.

As we described already, the factors that leaders tend to overlook are related to the people involved in the project: management, end users, and stakeholders. Each of the seven levers interacts in some way with these three groups of people.

Who Is Who?

Earlier we explained some of the common jargon in digital transformations. Our findings, which we discuss next, are based on nuanced questions. In these questions, we tried to simplify the complex realities of digital transformations, but we were pretty specific.

When we talk about *the transformation*, we refer to everybody involved and impacted by the organizational change. When we refer to *the project*, we mean the core team of internal and external experts assembled to deliver the change.

Every project has a start and a finish,[1] which makes projects *temporary organizations*. The transformation aims to make changes to the organization that started the project. We refer to this as the *permanent organization*.

We examine management specifically in Chapter 7. At this point, it is most important to understand that management represents the leaders and decision-makers of the permanent organization. The leadership of the transformation – the consultants and experts necessary to realize the change – forms a temporary organization.

Naturally, every organization has many managers. To simplify, we think of management as falling into three categories:

1. *Frontline management* – the people who are the direct managers of the employees who do the work that is changing.
2. *Middle management*—the next level up from frontline management. Again, in most organizations, this is a large group of employees. Yet, because they are well connected downward and upward in the organization, they often are great force multipliers in communication – one middle manager can spread information a long way across the organization with comparatively little effort.
3. *Top management* – the senior leadership of the organization. These are the leaders who often set strategy and govern change efforts. You typically will find top management on your transformation's steering committee – the committee convened to make the most senior decisions about the transformation.

End Users

The end users are those who do the actual work daily. Naturally, they will be most impacted by the changes in systems or processes – the end users actually need to change their behaviors or attitudes as a direct reaction to the technology change.

While often end users are the organization's workers, employees, and team members, this does depend on the nature of the organization or the systems; sometimes end users are not part of the permanent organization. Rather, they are clients, customers, or even citizens.

We debated for a long time what we should call the people who do the work and whose working lives will change. Much strategic thinking and planning about transformations focuses on how organizations introduce new ways of thinking, acting, and operating. Yet organizations are made up of people, and people are not passive. The worst phrasing we encountered is "change recipients."

As we describe later, such a framing suggests a passive role, yet these users are, after all, the most critical group of people to make change successful. In a similar vein, we frequently hear the phrase "resistance to change." Psychologists have long established that this is not a helpful way of framing; "How do we overcome resistance to change?" is the wrong question to respond to. A better framing of the question is: "How do we build commitment to change?"

After much debate, we settled on the term "end users," borrowing from language typical in IT projects and information systems development. End users must understand and commit to the change, even if they are not the intended beneficiaries.

Workers will use only those systems that they can understand or support. Clients or customers who feel inconvenienced by the change will complain. If end users reject the new systems or processes, the transformation will fail, as much as it would have if the technology did not work.

Stakeholders

Typically, we think of stakeholders as anyone who has a stake in the transformation's success. Stakeholders are those individuals without whose support the transformation itself cannot succeed. Stakeholders make or break the change just as much as end users do, but for different reasons and at different stages of the transformation.

End users work with the new systems, processes, and ways of working that change will bring. Management organizes, plans, coordinates, and directs the work of end users.

Stakeholders are the ones whose blessing or approval is vital in starting and running the transformation.

While the term "stakeholders" could include workers and employees or customers and clients, their role here is different from that of end users. Stakeholders also include those in charge of controlling the funding, resources, and direction of the company – such as shareholders or C-suite executives, unions, regulators, auditors, and others.

Successfully convincing stakeholders to support a transformation ensures that the team will receive the resources, funding, and goodwill to complete it.

What Are the Seven Levers for Success?

Having defined the types of people that a digital transformation might need to consider, what *are* the seven levers?

1. *A clear reason for change* – Very few organizations will risk the time, effort, and cost of a digital transformation for no reason at all. There will almost always be a reason behind the transformation. However, the organization's motives and interests are not always the same as those of its end users and stakeholders. How important is it for the organization and management to make the reasons for change clear and relatable to end users or stakeholders?

2. *Defined approach to managing change* – A transformation is a significant undertaking. Beginning a transformation without having planned and clarified the precise approach for managing change down to the last detail is idiotic. How exactly does detailed change planning interact with

the planned technology development? What level of planning change activities will benefit the implementation? What should a good plan look like, and can you do too much planning?

3. *Early involvement of users* – Often the people in charge of implementing a digital transformation are programmers and designers who will never be the end users simply because end users do not have the expertise or knowledge to design and program the systems that solve the organization's problems. But do programmers and designers need to involve end users? How vital are end users in designing and testing processes and systems? What should that involvement look like, and how early should users be involved?

4. *Management ownership* – Management both represents the organization's goals and is accountable for realizing the benefits. However, management contains several groups with different levels of authority and responsibility: top, middle, and frontline. What role do top, middle, and frontline managers play in successful change? What does taking ownership of change look like?

5. *Effective communication* – There needs to be communication for management, stakeholders, and end users to cooperate. Change cannot happen without active and deliberate communication. What needs to be considered for this communication to be effective?

6. *Effective training* – A lot of work and effort goes into developing and implementing new systems. However, this effort is wasted if end users do not understand how these systems work. What can be done to ensure that the training is effective, and how early in the life cycle of the transformation as a whole should training be considered?

7. *Trust-based relationships* – People make or break change. This lever is about establishing and maintaining productive relationships between end users and stakeholders regarding the transformation and the project implementation. Having strong relationships based on the trust of end users and stakeholders affects the success of the transformation. What factors build this trust in the project?

Testing the Seven Levers

In our interviews, we collected data that allowed us to test the seven levers of change.

For levers #5 and #6 (effectiveness of communication and training), we asked a single question on a 10-point scale. We measured early user involvement by the time it took for users to become involved. The defined approach was a simple yes/no question. For the other levers, we combined multiple questions into one factor, and we present detailed statistics in Appendix B. In our interviews, we asked follow-up questions to get more detailed explanations.

To identify which of these seven levers is associated with success or failure, we combined the perspectives of success (project management, people, benefits, and results) discussed in Appendix B into one overall success factor.

We then tested our success formula, as shown in Figure 3.1. The formula shows the results of testing our success formula with real-world data from the 155 transformations. The graph shows the estimated effects in the regression model. For each of the seven levers (shown on the vertical axis), the horizontal axis shows the mean strength of the effect (dot) and the 95% confidence interval of the effect estimate (whiskers around the dots).

If a lever's effect is zero, then it has no effect. Figure 3.2 shows that this is the case for lever #3, early end user involvement, a finding that surprised us and that we unpack in Chapter 6. For levers #1 and #2 (clear vision and defined change approach), the 95% confidence interval includes zero. Our data are inconclusive for these levers; the effect is not statistically significant, and we cannot rule out that they do not have an impact.

The remaining levers – #4 Management ownership, #5 Effective communication, #6 Effective training, and #7 Trust-based relationships – have a statistically significant effect. If we sort them from most impactful to least impactful on success, we find that our success formula for change is:

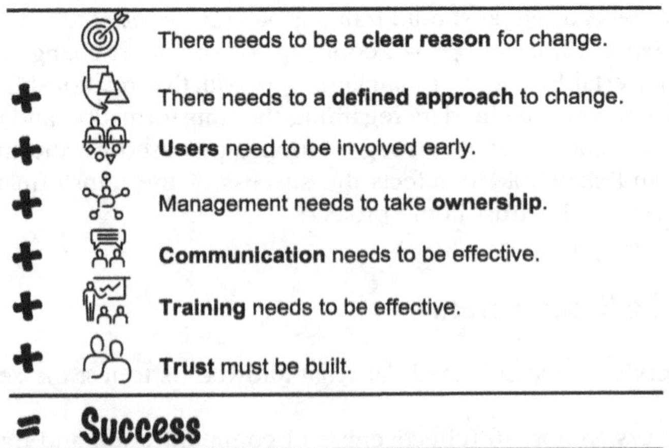

FIGURE 3.1 The hypothesized success formula for digital transformation based on our systematic literature review and validation workshops with experts.

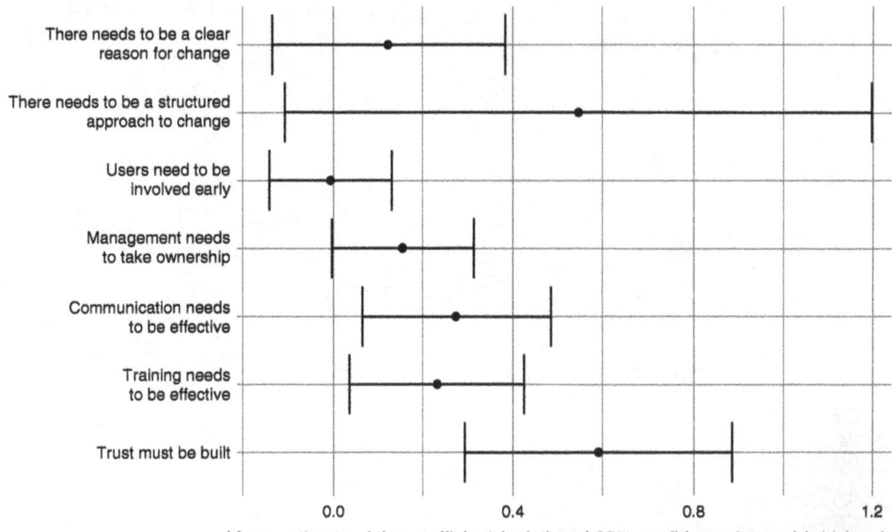

FIGURE 3.2 Coefficient plot for the regression model fitted to the data showing the mean estimate of the effect size of the coefficient (points) and the 95% Bayesian confidence interval (whiskers). The effect is insignificant when zero is included in the confidence intervals.

> Digital Transformation Success = Trust-based relationships + Effective communication + Effective training + Management ownership

It surprised us that a clear vision (Lever #1), a defined change approach (Lever #2), and early end user involvement (Lever #3) had no statistically significant association with success. In the next chapters, we examine each lever in turn to explore why this is the case.

CHAPTER 4

Lever #1: Clear Reason for Change

Any framework for change management will tell you that you need a clear reason for any transformation. As a result, organizations invest time and energy into defining the overall story and vision behind the transformation. Our research suggests that having a clear vision does not directly impact transformation success statistically. Further analysis of our data found an indirect effect, however.

Frameworks for managing change often start at the top management level of the organization, which creates a "vision" that clarifies the purpose behind the change and allows the "why," "how," and "what" of the change to be explained and followed up on.

Why might we not find a statistically significant link between the clear reason for change and the success of transformation?

First, we have observed in our interviews that the benefit to the permanent organization and the vision of its top management is not necessarily one that translates well to end users and stakeholders. Often the project team expends a great deal of effort into establishing a vision, mission statement, and reasons for change, only for it to become clear that there are more pragmatic reasons to change that would appeal to end users and stakeholders more.

An example could be an IT system that has gone out of support. Without support and updates, this system now represents a cybersecurity risk and is out of date. This IT system needs to be updated or replaced. From the organization's perspective, it is a clear and obvious decision – while there may not be any tangible benefits or significant change of function, the improved security is invaluable.

End users do not directly experience these benefits; however, the system they were familiar with is now being changed. They need to adapt to a new interface and possibly new processes. If they do not know the reason behind the change, they will get frustrated – the new system they need to use represents inconvenience only with no offered benefits.

Notoriously, customer relationship management sales system implementations often fail for this reason. Individual salespeople might not experience direct benefits from the new processes. Their role drives them to value their time; time wasted cuts into their performance and limits their bonus. Because adjusting to a new system takes time, salespeople will stick with the system that is familiar and works for them rather than waste time adjusting.

A clear reason for the transformation is valuable only if the organization can successfully translate this reason into some form of rationale or benefit to those it affects. Without this, those affected have no personal reason to accept the change or trust that it is necessary. When this translation happens successfully, it helps align the attitude of the organization, its stakeholders, and its end users toward the transformation.

Case Study: Supermarket

[Kim] An example is a Danish supermarket that made an app viral. Management saw an opportunity in this success to get a competitive advantage by building on this app to break into the digital market. The IT team was tasked with putting this digital transformation into action.

However, management should have spent more effort aligning employees with this change. In this case, the bewildered employees got left behind. While their employer started to lean into the digital angle – presenting the company as software vendors and providers – the employees still considered themselves to be working for a supermarket.

In the end, this supermarket chain has achieved little benefit for its customers, the shoppers, despite its heavy investments in IT and digital systems; its vision of achieving a competitive advantage has failed.

This scenario, however, is not the worst-case one. In the 1990s, the American retailer Kmart failed to embrace new technological advances that its competitor, Walmart, had been investing heavily in. Walmart had invested so heavily in technology that it was the first private-sector company to own a satellite controlling the flow of digital information between its supermarkets and head office, for example.

When Walmart began dominating the market, Kmart struggled to keep up. Fundamentally, at all levels of the organization, Kmart employees considered themselves retailers. Their core competencies were marketing and promotion. Digital and technological transformations were supposed to be something other than a core capability of the organization.

> Kmart's struggles grew when the industry shifted, and digital technologies became central to retailers' business models. Kmart lacked a clear strategic motive for embracing technology. In the end, Kmart's attempts at digital transformations were unsuccessful, contributing to the company's bankruptcy in 2002.[1]

Two Approaches to Defining the Reason for the Change

Commonly, two narratives emerge in this translation: "We need to fix a burning platform" and "We seek a pot of gold." The difference between the narratives lies in avoiding the negative pain point or chasing the positive reward.

The admittedly dramatic concept of a "burning platform" wants you to imagine that you are standing on a burning oil platform in the sea. The reason to act is apparent – stay on the platform and die or jump into the water and live. In business, a burning platform presents why the status quo cannot be maintained – without change, a bad thing will turn worse.

The phrase was coined in Daryl R. Conner's analysis of the 1988 Piper Alpha disaster.[2] A fire on the oil rig in the North Sea claimed 167 deaths, making it one of the worst offshore catastrophes in history. One of the 62 survivors of the fire, Andrew Mochan, said that he jumped off the rig not because he knew he would be saved but because he knew that all other options were certain death.[3]

A typical example of the burning platform in digital transformations is outdated software that creates cybersecurity vulnerabilities. The change or inconvenience is justified by explaining that the upgrades will prevent hackers from attacking the system; the resulting damage to the organization might have put jobs at risk.

A burning platform's more cheerful opposite, the pot of gold, makes you imagine the hunt for gold at the end of the rainbow: find something that is unquestionably helpful and good. Here, the reason to act is to achieve the reward. Suppose the supermarket going digital wanted to present its confused employees with a pot-of-gold incentive. In that case, management might have explained how becoming a software vendor would increase profits and allow for employee raises.

Our data (see Figure 4.1 and Appendix B) show no apparent link with success, whether your vision is a pot of gold, a fix of a burning platform, or both. In fact, we found that in about one-third of the transformations, the vision had elements of both a burning platform and a pot of gold. The rest of the transformations were pretty evenly split among having a vision centered around a pot of gold, the fix of a burning platform, or neither.

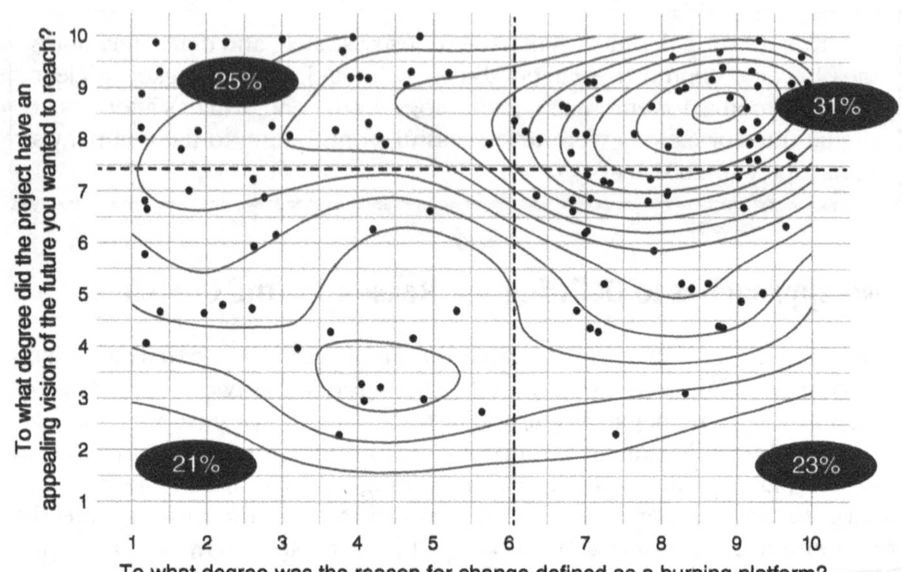

FIGURE 4.1 The narratives for change in our data.

Conner suggested a helpful two-by-two grid to develop your narrative for change. The grid adds a second dimension to the distinction between the burning platform and the pot of gold. The organization's current state and the anticipated future can also be problematic or full of opportunities (Figure 4.2).

	Burning Platform	Pot of Gold
Current	We are in trouble now	We can take advantage of this situation by acting now
Anticipated	We are going to be in trouble	If we prepare now, we can profit from the situation in the future

FIGURE 4.2 Narratives for change.
Source: Adapted from Conner, 1992, *Managing at the speed of change.*

What Limits the Ability to Translate Vision?

Finding reasons to support and accept change is easy at face value. Top management in headquarters or the project managers in the IT department will usually be able to think of a long list of great reasons that promise endless benefits. However, these reasons often fail to land correctly.

They fail because tailoring the reason for the change is hard work and requires understanding the daily environment in which a solution is supposed to operate. With this awareness and understanding, it is easier to make the vision relatable. Some of the time spent in vision workshops might be better spent going out into the field and asking the people implementing and affected by the change for help in the translation.

One good way to present a pot of gold is through simulations and prototypes. Once the anticipated benefits have been physically demonstrated, they are much easier to see and trust. In addition to wireframes and mockups, presenting real-life testimonies from colleagues and other end users describing their positive experiences is helpful.

A more granular approach is valuable instead of creating one grand vision for the entire organization. The grand vision risks being too vague or abstract for the specific end users, which means that it is valuable to target specific groups of end users individually – tailoring a vision for change to each group.

It becomes easier to tailor the vision when project managers clearly understand how a specific group of end users benefits from the change through conducting field interviews. Understanding each specific context enables the creation of a particular vision that is uniquely focused and motivational in a way that a unified grand vision never could be.

Case Study: North Sea Oil Rigs

[Kim] A client we work with deals in oil and gas. We were hired to help develop a communication strategy as part of a transformation rolling out an enterprise resource planning upgrade. The first part of our work was to go to oil rigs in the North Sea and other parts of the world to interview users, asking them what they wanted.

When we started the digital transformation, we really tried to live up to what the users told us. They told us that they didn't want communication. Ultimately, they didn't trust headquarters – they felt their work was going well and so didn't need anything else. They had become fed up

(continued)

(continued)

with promises about great benefits from previously announced changes that never resembled what they eventually got.

The communications they were getting generally were totally unaware of the reality on the oil rigs. As a result, headquarters' attempts to translate management's visions and make the vision relatable were completely off-target and actually built mistrust rather than inspiring confidence and commitment to the changes.

A particularly amusing example concerned a training video that had utterly failed to do its research and understand its audience. In this video, a man obviously intended to represent the workers – being particularly rough and rugged while dressed in full personal protective equipment and safety gear – explained and demonstrated the new system in action.

Throughout the video and his presentation, he moved around the oil rig, performing regular duties and acting out an everyday routine. One such routine was eating lunch, where he was shown with his hard hat on the table beside his plate. The workers immediately smelled a rat – you never put your hard hat next to your food when eating.

This small detail showed that the video's creators completely lacked awareness of the processes that made up workers' lives, destroying the video's credibility. Even worse, this split-second scene became emblematic of the us-versus-them culture rift between the head office and local workers.

The effect was like an elderly teacher trying to relate to teenagers by dressing like them and copying their slang. The apparent differences in experience and lifestyle drown out any possible relatability the message might have had.

In the end, the implications of our interviews for crafting a better communication strategy were straightforward. Workers did not want to be disturbed if at all possible. If communication was needed, it must be meaningful for the workers. If users have no reason to believe a change is relevant to them and because they had little trust in headquarters, they want nothing to do with any changes made to the enterprise resource planning system.

One way of making the communication relatable and compelling was to make the management itself relatable and sympathetic to the frontline staff – recontextualizing the conversation from frontline versus head office to users versus problem. For example, having the CEO stand up and stress that they, too, were frustrated users of the system really resonated with the frontline staff.

Creating the Translation Together

Successfully translating the organization's vision into one relevant to end users and stakeholders has one simple rule: Those affected by the change should have input.

In our interviews, we heard repeatedly that an organization's employees not only value but also expect to be part of the co-creation process. This collaboration allows you to ensure that the message gets across without any miscommunications getting in the way.

Another approach is testing suggested translations of the organization's vision on focus groups. By having these groups provide feedback on the messaging, you can identify what is successful and what is not. A focus group would likely have caught the mistake in the promotional video with the hard hat on the table.

Management Buy-in

Another resource for creating and passing on a relatable vision is middle and frontline management. Frontline management will be the most regular point of contact between end users and the organization. In contrast, middle management often presents a smaller, more manageable group of people who are fantastic force multipliers in communication.

By helping end users buy into and understand the transformation, managers can become your biggest advocates, presenting the benefits of the change to their team members in a relatable way.

The key issue, however, as we explain in Chapter 7, is that managers often need to know what exactly they need to do to own the change. So, according to our insights, the role of a project should be to enable managers, through guidance, tools, and training, to engage their teams in the vision co-creation process and feed back into the consolidated effort.

Throughout the transformation, management should operate as a source of support for end users. If management understanding of the vision, the reason for the change, and how to make these relatable to the end users can help facilitate this support.

A transformation we have worked with has actively incentivized managers to support and promote the transformation in this way. In fact, we collaborated on building a financial incentive model for middle managers, encouraging them to help with the change. In doing this, we created a source of support and guidance for both end users and frontline managers in promoting the change process.

What Do the Data Say?

We failed to find a direct link in the data between a clear vision for change and success. In our interviews, we also heard that co-creation is the expectation – thus, a clear and polished top-management vision is detrimental to success. We then analyzed the complex network of effects to identify second-order effects.

Figure 4.3 shows our data-driven explanation, which shows the complex role of creating a clear reason for the change to make the transformation successful. Only the statistically significant direct and indirect effects are

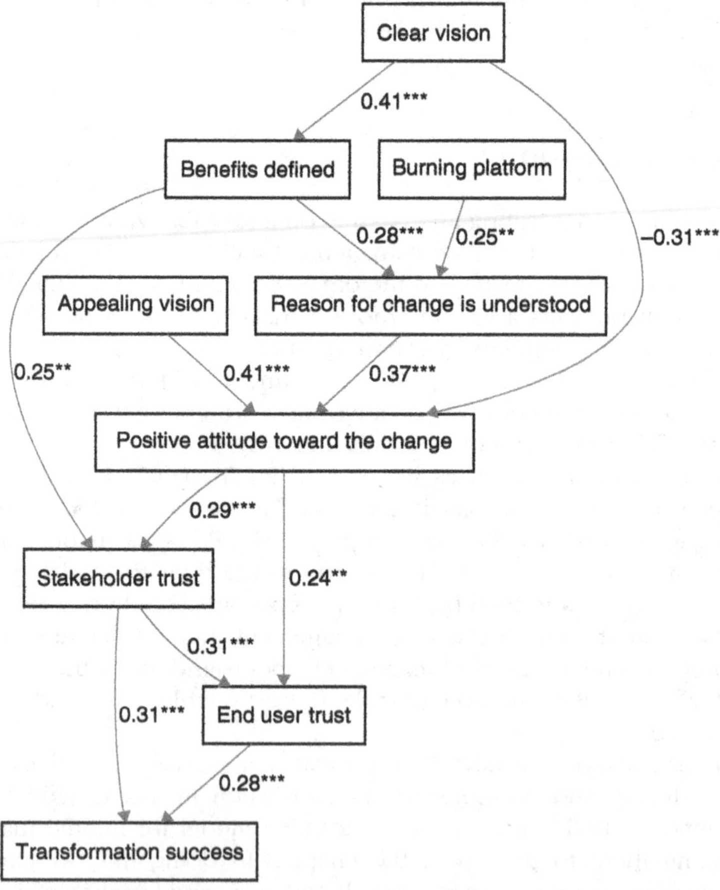

FIGURE 4.3 The pathways between clarity of the vision for the change and transformation success.

shown in this figure. Also shown are the standardized effect sizes for these statistically significant effects, which range from 0 to 1, allowing us to compare the different strengths of the effects.

In nontechnical terms, Figure 4.3 shows how an apparent reason and characteristics associated with envisioning a transformation drive success. In short, the data tell us that the key is trust, and an evident reason builds trust in the change and the project.

The first pathway we identified was that a clear vision helps define the transformation's benefits. Better benefits definition increases stakeholder trust, which has a direct and statistically significant impact on the success of the technology transformation. We explore trust in more detail in Chapter 10, but a key takeaway from our analysis is that clearly aligned mutual benefits are a major factor in building trust.

The second pathway was balancing the pot-of-gold and burning platform visions. The data showed that defined benefits and the degree to which the reason for the change is a burning platform improve end users' understanding of the reason for the change. The pot-of-gold story (or appealing vision) and the knowledge of why the change is necessary improve users' positive attitude toward the change.

A positive attitude toward change and an understanding of why change is necessary create a commitment to change. In turn, a positive attitude toward change increases trust by stakeholders and end users in the transformation, which is the primary driver of success.

However, a *very* clear vision decreases this positive attitude toward the change. The first critical insight is that a vision might be too abstract for many stakeholders and end users. Yet a very clear vision is also useful. A clear vision helps the transformation to be much more specific about the benefits and reasons for the change, which helps build trust.

So, in short, we find that a clear vision enables better management of benefits, and the vision – if co-created – is instrumental in specifying more clearly the benefits and reason for change and for building trust.

Cultural Influences on Change

These approaches to translating and communicating a relatable vision to end users and stakeholders are not one-size-fits-all. For example, our earlier example of providing a financial incentive to management, such as overtime pay for working for change activities and training delivery, would work only in organizations in which motivations are money-driven. Organizations with different values and cultures will need different approaches.

Case Study: Accommodating Cultural Differences

[Kim] My experience can serve as an extreme example of how cultural differences can impact communication. We were working on a project for an international pharmaceutical company with facilities in Denmark and China. We had to deal and communicate the reasons behind the project in completely different ways for each facility.

We were touring the client's operations worldwide, laying the groundwork for a three-year project. We met with as many employees as possible to explain the reasoning behind the project and answer any questions or concerns.

In the Danish branch, we invited all employees to come to our presentation and then dialogue with us about the new project. This event was extremely successful – we had very high attendance and some lively debate about the project.

In the Chinese branch, we repeated the same process. However, hours before the presentation was due to kick off, only five workers had signed up. While all of the management was in attendance, there would be little benefit with so few workers there. We needed worker input.

So we turned to management for help. We explained that this meeting and presentation were an essential part of building the communication and training strategy that would help the project succeed and convinced management that worker attendance was necessary.

A few hours later, we had not 5 workers but 120 in attendance. The workshop was very successful in the end, and we got a vast amount of feedback on what our Chinese workers believed would make this a good project.

We learned that we had to be aware of and respect cultural differences between workplaces. The approach to sharing vision and motivating end users and stakeholders will vary between workplaces and countries; just because a motivational approach works in one branch does not mean it will work in another.

In the Chinese branch, a top-down approach was far more effective. Once management was on board, they were able to motivate employees to engage as needed. Once managers understood the reasoning, they were able to co-create the vision for the changes without our help; in fact, without this intervention – the employees saw no reason to interact with us.

However, the top-down approach was less effective in the Danish branch. Employees needed a more personal touch from us. As they were more willing to challenge the reasoning for the change that would have

> motivated their managers, we needed to interact more closely with them from the start.
>
> These differences in culture required vastly different approaches from us. Our assumption that what the Danish branch had found motivational would work for the Chinese branch meant that we initially failed until we adjusted to recognize the best way to motivate the people we were dealing with at that moment.

Our key takeaways on how to craft a clear reason for change are:

- *Don't* create the perfect, polished top-management vision. This does the opposite of what we expected – it creates questioning of the change and the project established to deliver the change, making success harder to achieve.
- *Do* co-create the vision with users. Co-creation of the vision is not nice to have. It's expected.
- *Don't* try to involve every member of the organization in the co-creation process. Practically, the most promising approaches are focus groups and using middle and frontline managers as multipliers.
- *Do* use the vision to identify the benefits better and enable more successful project management.
- *Don't* rely on a single narrative type. Use a balanced vision comprising elements of the pot-of-gold and the burning platform narratives. The former creates a positive attitude toward the change, and the latter makes the logical reasons for change more straightforward to understand.
- *Do* tailor the approach to fit the organization's norms and expectations.

CHAPTER 5

Lever #2: Defined Approach to Managing Change

A common belief we encountered in our research – in our interviews with organizations, workshops with change experts, and other studies – is that having a defined approach to managing change is essential. A "defined approach" means having a framework or guiding structure to plan and organize organizational change activities.

Sixty-five percent of the digital transformations we interviewed claimed to have a defined approach. Most commonly, this meant that transformations planned their communications, user training, or how to involve users:

- 40% of the transformations we studied took this approach, mainly in this order: planning communication, then planning training, then user involvement.
- 24% of the transformations relied on a classic waterfall approach, which meant that they defined workstreams and milestones for their change activities.
- 13% of transformations followed change frameworks developed by the organization. These frameworks were based on popular ones from consultants and academics.[1]
- 10% of transformations structured their approach by clearly defining the outcomes to be achieved and then organized the execution with a focus on benefits realization.
- 7% of transformations used frameworks from the agile and design thinking toolkits.
- The remaining 6% used other frameworks, such as principles of learning organization, social work, and social change.

As discussed in Chapter 1, a common issue with having a defined approach to change is that often there is too much focus on planning and less on action. As a result, often there are significant investments of time and money to hire consultants and specialists to develop very detailed and specific plans, but the plans quickly fall apart – amounting to lovely ideas on paper only.

Indeed, in our data, only half the transformations (51%) stuck to their defined approach for change. The problem with having such a defined approach to managing change is that the change itself is subject to all kinds of unpredictable changes. Why?

Humans are fundamentally unpredictable beings. Since change management involves working with humans, unpredictable changes and adjustments to the transformation are inevitable. Managing change is a wicked problem.

Figure 5.1 explains how two types of complexity impact organizational change. On one hand, we find the behavioral complexity that stems from working with humans. On the other hand, we have the dynamics of working in complex systems.

Organizational change is not a "tame" problem free of the complexities of working with humans and complex systems. A scientific approach works only in tame issues. Tame issues, for example, might be purely technical projects, such as upgrades of a database or a server or similar IT projects that go unnoticed by users.

When managing change, we work in areas of high behavioral complexity: Stakeholders are not automatically aligned; goals and objectives are ill defined and conflict with each other; and, sometimes, we do not even know what the problem is.

In addition, we work with the complexity of dynamic systems. The permanent organization – the business – will not stop changing to adjust to the needs and demands of the industry while the transformation is ongoing. At the same time, the temporary organization – the team implementing the project – might be adjusting to the demands of the transformation and

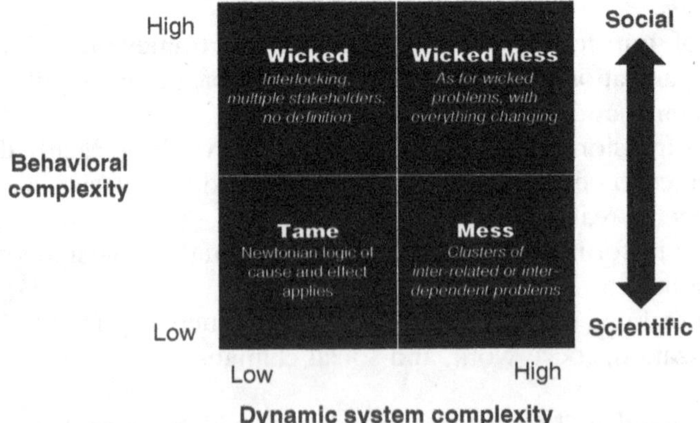

FIGURE 5.1 Complexity of change – why change is a wicked problem.

technology itself. Besides, in any complex organization, we have a limited understanding of cause and effects; some minor changes have the fabled butterfly effect of creating surprising and unintended impacts.

Working on wicked problems or even wicked messes – where the situation changes constantly – has significant consequences for defining an approach to managing change: Scientific solutions (if … then … else) do not work. Our approaches must work with humans and their unpredictability and tendency to change their minds. Finally, the insights from wicked problems tell us that a perfect solution does not exist. Thus, any approach needs to retain flexibility as we understand the transformation better.

What Is the Benefit of Having a Defined Approach?

Although in our studies, a clearly defined approach did not significantly impact the success of the implementation, it had a crucial indirect effect on the success of the transformation.

The data show that a top-down, waterfall-style approach delivers the project within budget and schedule but is ineffective in achieving transformation success in terms of people, benefits, and overall results.

However, the data also show that leaders who present a clearly defined approach to managing the change are far more successful in securing something vital to the transformation's success – dedicated resources and budget. With dedicated resources and budget, the team will have the people, time, and funding required to manage the organizational change.

When to Stop Defining Your Approach

When it comes to defining the approach, we have discovered two things. First, as has been discussed throughout the book, action needs to start as early as possible; planning without effective action is a waste of time and resources. Second, the primary benefit and impact of having a strongly defined approach to managing change is that it helps secure the resources and funding to carry out the transformation.

The question then becomes: How do you know when to stop planning and start acting? Because change is a wicked problem, no perfect, scientific answers to this question exist. Before taking the next step, we need to understand what is good enough for now. It is not easy to put a precise measure or definable milestone on when one activity ends and another starts; every transformation and organization will have different needs and requirements. However, both should exist in balance – planning and acting should not exclude the other.

From our findings, we conclude that it is necessary to:

- Focus on resource requirements.
- Keep the benefits and results being achieved in focus.
- Develop a plan to pull the other six levers described in this book.

If planning offers no benefits but is done merely for the sake of having a detailed plan, it might be time to start acting.

Thinking from Right to Left

One leader told us we must "think from the right to the left and then execute from the left to the right." They meant that we should start thinking and planning with the end goal in mind (the goal that sits on the right of the Gantt chart – the timeline – of any project). Execution later focuses on left-to-right thinking, which means taking one step after another.

So, what is on the right of your timeline? If your systems are outdated, carrying out a digital transformation "To update our systems to be cutting edge" is an intimidatingly vague and overwhelming goal.

In a workshop where we collected current best practices for benefit realization in digital transformations, we found that the best approach was to be focused and specific. The better transformations avoid the trap of trying to boil the ocean by aiming to achieve all the potential benefits at once. Rather, they focus on up to four or five specific and low-level processes that the new system will support.

A proposed transformation phrased as "Our finance management system will be able to perform these four specific functions more efficiently" often provides enough cost savings to justify spending of up to 300 million USD, for example.

An important part to remember is the lesson shared by one project leader: "Never let the engineers name your project!" Framing the purpose of the transformation is essential. Very few people get excited about working hard to cut costs and lay off employees.

Framing the Purpose of the Transformation

Ørsted is a market-leading Danish company in renewable energy. The organization's transformation journey from a state-owned oil and gas company into a leader in renewables is impressive.

> Equally impressive is how Ørsted transformed the way offshore wind farms are built. In the seven years between 2012 and 2018, Ørsted engineers reduced the cost of building and operating an offshore wind park by 63%.[2] However, they did not do this by setting out the ambition to cut costs; – few engineers would get out of bed to make things cheaper.
>
> The organization's leaders set the challenge in this way: "We need to build an offshore wind farm in 10 months, which is the weather window for construction in the North Sea." The cost reduction then followed.

In our research, we found some digital transformations that used the jobs-to-be-done framework.[3] The model has been embraced by the design thinking community as the value proposition,[4] which asks: What job does this technology do in our organization?

The jobs-to-be-done framework encourages left-to-right thinking by first asking what job a user hires a technology solution to do. Then it asks: Where are the pains and what are the gains with the current solution?

In digital transformations, the question must also be asked at the organizational level. What is the job to be done that this company hires this system for?

Sometimes answering for the company is less intuitive than answering for the user. Perhaps the technology is not outdated; rather, the role of IT within the organization is not defined in a way that provides a competitive advantage. These days, an organization's IT capabilities are not just back-office functions that support the business; IT offers capabilities that put the organization ahead of its competitors.

In some cases, digital transformation meant that the organization developed a technology-led business model, changed to a platform-centric business model, or restructured the business operations around user journeys.

We have seen significant returns on investment in transformations that did not necessarily involve writing a line of code to update old systems or provide new tools. Instead, the company redefined and reconsidered its role in IT and digital solutions. Establishing clarity about the technical support the organization needs and where its digital capabilities place it in the competitive landscape makes long-term future benefits and results possible.

Table 5.1 shows the findings from interviewing 45 technology experts on the best-case – yet realistic – expected benefits from a digital transformation and the typical cost for that type of transformation.[5] The figure also shows the benefit-to-cost ratio.

What is surprising is that big transformations, such as exiting and replacing outdated systems, are costly and provide relatively small cost savings. The benefit-to-cost ratio is only 0.17, meaning these transformations typically

TABLE 5.1 Estimated cost and benefits of digital transformations.

Area	Specific transformations	Benefits (maximum cost savings as % of total annual IT spend)	Cost for typical transformation (as % of total IT cost)	Benefit/ Cost ratio
Large-scale technology change	Strategy to exit and manage legacy systems	25%	150%	0.17
	Establishing digital data architecture	19%	75%	0.25
	Moving toward composable architecture	12%	25%	0.48
Role of technology in business	Technology-centered business strategy	49%	10%	4.90
	Streamlined governance	32%	5%	6.40
	Integrated business technology management	32%	10%	3.20
Technology delivery	High levels of automation	31%	25%	1.24
	Right location mix	26%	10%	2.60
	Demand management optimization	26%	5%	5.20

have a payback period of six years. Compare that to transforming the technology governance (benefit-to-cost ratio of 6.4) or better demand management (5.2), which offer much quicker returns.

By clarifying what job is done by the technology, in addition to the pain points and gains experienced by users, it is possible to understand better the technology's role in the organization and how to align end users and stakeholders with the change. Understanding the activities required to align users and stakeholders with the change, in turn, allows for the more effective planning of activities for the transformation to reduce the pain points while maximizing the gains.

A better understanding of the jobs-to-be-done by the technology could lead to very different solutions. Instead of a systems replacement, the transformation could be anything from reimagining how the company uses its available resources to discovering that currently implemented processes could be optimized.

An example is a large European bank that redefined technology's role in the organization. The bank's goal was to enter the Spanish market without opening a single branch.

Recognizing the power of apps in banking, the bank reconfigured its new customers' journey, removing the need to visit a branch to open an account. Instead, new customers just need to fill out an application through an app and book a time and place the next day. At the time and location of their choice, they will receive all necessary documentation, cards, PIN numbers, and authentication devices via courier within 24 hours of their application – all with only one customer signature required.

The bank's service was dramatically improved by redefining how its existing technology is used without costly investments in new technology. By embracing the benefits of mobile apps – improved user flexibility and freedom – the bank was able to make the complex process of opening a new account far more user-friendly and successfully entered a new European market.

Is "Classic" Change Management Obsolete?

The traditional approach to change management is usually a linear top-down method, famously described by Kotter in 1995.[6] The CEO or another member of top management has a vision and then cascades the vision down from the top.

The result is a waterfall structure that resembles industrial megaprojects,[7] which shareholders are typically familiar with and reasonably good at managing.

In the early stages, waterfall megaprojects start with defining the benefits and outcomes. Then projects are translated into user requirements, with the development of tangible and intangible deliverables that satisfy the user requirements. A plan of activities and inputs required to create the deliverables is created, and, finally, everything is costed up.

This traditional approach aims to plan a project until the design is perfect and frozen; then the execution begins. A milestone at the end strictly defines each phase; you cannot revisit and change the plan or design once development has started, for example.

This approach has benefits. Our data show that it is particularly effective in securing budget and resources and finishing the transformation within budget and deadlines. However, here is the crux: While a great top-down plan helps get stakeholders on board and the digital transformation funded, the reality is starkly different.

A rigid top-down approach does not account for the nature of change and organizational change management; as discussed earlier, these are wicked problems, not tame ones. Digital transformations tend not to be as rigid in structure as industrial megaprojects.[8]

Identifying and designing the ideal solution may take time, and the milestones might need to shift and adapt over time. In our interviews, we heard a common challenge for transformation leaders: the project took a more flexible approach – design thinking (e.g., agile or lean), where the basic idea is the rapid iteration of prototypes and experiments, yet the organization controlled all its investments conventionally through defined milestones and progress toward milestones.

Keeping the intended result in mind is essential, as is not letting the planning phase hold back action. Considering alternative approaches to defining and planning is also valuable.

Alternate Approaches to Planning

The emergency services and military have an approach known as capability-based planning, which differs dramatically from rigid, process-driven approaches.[9] Rather than identifying what actions need to be taken and in which sequence, capability-based planning asks what kind of experts do we need here? Once those experts are in place, organizations trust the expert's training and experience to deliver the outcome and adapt during execution as needed.

From a change management perspective, capability-based planning would involve identifying the problem to be solved using scenario planning and the skill sets required. The levers for success we discuss in this book could be good headlines for the required capabilities. In digital transformations, in addition to technical people, individuals would be needed who are skilled at communication and training, at managing, at user involvement, and in building of trust.

If done correctly, the transformation will run more smoothly and be naturally more flexible. When subject-matter experts are available, they can coordinate and structure how they approach their aspect of the transformation more effectively, as they presumably understand their area better than the planner does. They also can adapt to changes as they arise, and the transformation evolves more flexibly.[10]

Case Study: Focusing the Plan on Technological Needs

[Alex] In one digital transformation, we used a twist on capability-based planning.

A healthcare provider needed to digitize the clinical screening tests offered to patients. The current process was based on letters, which meant that some patients missed their invitations to the tests and cancers were missed, with devastating outcomes for the patients.

The digitization of all screening tests seemed overwhelmingly complex. Lots of processes and versions of the same process existed. Different diseases have different processes. Many systems supported these processes, and the systems were not talking to each other.

We began by mapping the end-to-end patient journey for the most common screening tests. For example, we documented the journey to screen for breast cancer, a different process for liver cancer, a different one for diabetic eye conditions, and the like. A total of 14 different services existed, all operationally different and supported by different technology solutions.

Our next step was to identify commonalities, such as how people get invited to come for a test. How do they make appointments? How and where is the test conducted? Then we had to determine how they get the results. The journey also included some invisible commonalities to users, like identity verification or printing barcodes to stick on test tubes that go to a lab.

Next, we mapped the different variations in the services. Is this a screening test that gets triggered by the person's age? Is this a test initiated by a warning sign identified by the doctor? We looked at different types of tests: Do clinicians look at a scan? Do labs analyze blood?

The next step was to map out which journey elements are already supported by a technological solution. We looked at the solutions used across the 14 different services. We identified the ones everyone was happy with, the ones that needed minor improvements to commercial packages, and the elements that required new software development, and ended up with a clear tech architecture.

We then identified the screening service that needed to be fixed most urgently – the one with the largest number of papers and letters involved. We decided to start with the messiest screening service first because when we studied failed projects, a common misconception stood out. When asked for a minimum viable product, projects often choose what is easy. Yet, later on, more complex user journeys need to be added to the product, and then it all starts to fall apart.

Instead, we looked at different levels of the user journey: Do we need to track your test in the labs fully? Not initially, it can wait, but we need to be able to build it in. Do we integrate with the marketing tools to track the uptake of services and improve the communication strategy? Not initially, yet we need to be aware of it.

(continued)

(continued)

Ultimately, we ended up with a defined multiyear roadmap – making all these services entirely digital would take nearly 10 years. But we created a roadmap for the technology and the organizational changes required, the changes for the patients using the service, the frontline staff involved, and the tech teams who operate and maintain the systems that enable the new services.

Case Study: Focusing on What Offers the Most Benefit

[Tom] A plan we worked on that was practical and very well received by the client did not rely on a defined approach or action plan. Instead, it was a made-for-purpose description of what the organization would need regarding the change.

To make this description, we selected the five areas that, if the client focused on them, would allow them to get the greatest benefit from the project. I believe that the organization's management preferred this approach over the "classic" top-down defined approach as it offered specific, focused, and small tailor-made initiatives to follow.

Such an approach requires insight into the organization and its needs; however, gaining such insight can be a problem in the initial phases when investments need to be made. When top management start big transformations, the change project tends to default to be run exactly like the projects that went before.

Hybrid Models

Nithin Nohria and Michael Beer,[11] two professors at Harvard Business School, discussed the differences between top-down and bottom-up approaches to managing organizational change and developed a hybrid model for change. The insights from our interviews and research provide more nuance (Table 5.2).

Regarding *goals* of the change, the hybrid E+O model suggests that plans need to embrace the paradox between top-down – which is excellent at maximizing bottom-line impacts – and bottom-up, which is suited to building new organizational capabilities. Our research found that change does not have a singular goal. As discussed in Chapter 4, digital transformations need a clear idea of "What's in it for me?" for every stakeholder group. Goals are multifaceted, and that is how our interviewees practically embraced the paradox.

TABLE 5.2 Top-down and bottom-up approaches to managing change.

Dimension of change	Top-down (Theory E)	Bottom-up (Theory O)	Hybrid (Combined E+O)	Our insights
Reason for change	Maximize shareholder value	Develop organizational capability	Embrace paradox between economic value and organizational capability	Multifaceted "What's in it for me?"
Leadership	Manage change from the top	Encourage participation from the bottom-up	Set direction from the top and engage the people below	Transfer ownership of the change to all levels of hierarchy
Focus	Emphasize structure and systems	Build up corporate culture; employees; behavior and attitudes	Focus simultaneously on the hard (structure and systems) and the soft	Focus on the soft first, then the hard
Process	Plan and establish programs	Experiment and evolve	Plan for spontaneity	A portfolio of disciplined entrepreneurship (see Chapter 6)
Reward system	Motivate through financial incentives	Motivate through commitment use pay as fair exchange	Use incentives to reinforce but not drive change	Change as expectation in every job, celebrated but not incentivized as an extra responsibility
Use of consultants	Consultants analyze problems and shape solutions	Consultants support management in shaping their own solutions	Consultants are expert resources who empower employees	Experts are facilitators

Source: Adapted from Beer and Nohria (2000) with insights from our research on digital transformations.

Our insights also found that change *leadership* needs to occur at all levels of the organization and, notably, at the bottom – not just through engagement but also through actual ownership. We explain what that means in practice in detail in Chapter 7.

In Chapter 2, we discussed our insights that the change's focus must be on people first. We say this because digital transformations have a gravitational pull toward hard systems, such as technology or processes, that put into the background soft systems, like people, power, and politics. Our insights show that digital transformations need to prioritize the soft systems.

The *process* in the hybrid E+O model aims to plan for spontaneity. But how do you do this in practice? Many hybrids of waterfall and agile have emerged in digital transformations. In Chapter 6, we take a closer look at a model of disciplined entrepreneurship that offers a way of reconciling the differences based on what we learned in our research.

Finally, we need to reconsider the role of *incentives* and *consultants*. In our research, we did not hear about using cash incentives like bonus payments for change. When we explored what makes communication effective (Chapter 8) and the reason for change (Chapter 4), our critical insight was that managing change is something other than roles.

In all the cases we studied, the need to manage change at all levels of the organization was established as a given. As discussed in this chapter and further in Chapter 7, our findings indicate that consultants should act as facilitators. Considering consultants to be facilitators of change rather than consultants who analyze problems and make recommendations or consultants who shape solutions with the top management is a more practical perspective linked to transformation success.

Tailoring the Approach to the Organization

Whatever the approach taken, ensure that you keep things flexible. Our analysis of each lever to success has made it clear that it is important to revisit, adapt, and fine-tune throughout the project's life cycle; do not rigidly define an approach or strategy and never revisit or fine-tune it.

Processes such as communication, training, and management engagement need to be consistently followed up on and analyzed to measure their effectiveness. If feedback shows that they are not operating well, they need to be revisited and optimized immediately. Our new mantra is this: Make it more loopy! The other chapters explore the importance of building more feedback loops into digital transformations.

It's a common misconception that more flexible, bottom-up change approaches require less project management. In fact, they require more coordination, alignment, direction, planning, and replanning.

One reason why we need more coordination, alignment, direction, and planning and replanning is that change is not about scientific or industrial processes; it is about humans. Since humans are irrational, the approach taken to change cannot be purely rational. None of us is identical; we communicate, learn, and approach problems differently.

Designing your approach to be dynamic and adaptive to how the transformation evolves is essential. Indeed, our data show that the financial and time cost for project management rises with more adaptable approaches. In agile projects, the cost of project management was almost double that of project management in a rigidly defined top-down approach – 18% versus 10%.

Staying flexible requires a greater level of effort and resources. The data show that the key project management capabilities[12] to consider are how effective risk management is to allow the transformation to look forward and identify threats and opportunities that might impact the achievement of the transformation's objectives and how to create and maintain stakeholder alignment.

Part of the greater need for coordination might be ensuring trust between those in charge of managing the project and those in charge of managing the change. A project manager might prefer the structured linear approach, while the change manager requires more flexibility. Without the ability to coordinate and trade off as needed – relying on each other to cover their role – inevitable compromises arise that restrict the ability and performance of both teams.

Case Study: Attitudes to Change

[Alex] Marc Thompson, a colleague of mine at the University of Oxford, has a brilliant exercise on surfacing our assumptions about change. The purpose of this exercise is to uncover the different assumptions people have about organizational change, assumptions that affect how they approach that change. Understanding and balancing these approaches is necessary for productive teamwork and stakeholder buy-in.

Marc presents the class with a small case – the merger of two residential care providers for elderly persons and disabled persons. The class is divided into five groups and asked to come up with plans in 45 minutes on how to manage this merger.

Before the exercise, we surveyed the class to assess their beliefs and assumptions about change. Based on results of this survey, the groups are formed: People with similar beliefs and assumptions about change are in the same group.

After 45 minutes, we looked at what each group had produced. The result of assumptions at work are often eye-opening, particularly as the members of each group all have similar beliefs about change.

(continued)

(continued)

Group 1: *Change is about politics*. The focus in this group is typically on negotiation and reducing conflict. A lot of the planning and work here goes into identifying key stakeholders, who might be for or against the merger, and what could be offered in a negotiation.

Group 2: *Change requires a planned approach*. This group focuses on plans and actions to be taken. Participants might create a Gantt chart with milestones and key performance indicators and discuss how to implement and monitor the change. Participants also might discuss risk identification and how to adjust if the transformation evolves in certain directions.

Group 3: *Change is about people*. Here the focus is entirely on people. Participants might discuss skill sets and training or how to train specific abilities and skills. They will also discuss coordinating teams and their capacities.

Group 4: *Change is about learning*. This group is often about information. Students have identified essential questions and information to be discovered. They then discuss how to investigate their questions, gather the information, and then the steps to build on once the information has been acquired.

Group 5: *Change is complex*. The final group is often the most interesting to me, as there is nothing at all on the flipchart. Because these participants believe that change is uncertain and complex and that needed clarity is missing, they spend the entire 45 minutes in discussion. They usually get so focused on this that they do not write a single point down.

The key lesson we want the class to take away from this exercise is that every single group is right. Each group has a valid perspective on change; however, overemphasizing one perspective over the others unbalances the team's approach to the solution. All the perspectives should be balanced against each other to allow for a well-rounded picture. The same goes for your stakeholders – they expect to see different things.

Defining and Measuring the Progress of Change

Change management requires a flexible and adaptive approach, a fact that, unfortunately, makes defining concrete milestones difficult. It is not easy to specify a particular achievement or task as a fixed indicator of progress in a transformation that must be fluid in nature.

Setting fixed milestones works well in construction or industrial projects, as there is often a far more concrete deliverable and a very logical series of steps to be followed; after all, you cannot erect a roof before the walls are built, and neither can you test unwritten code. Change, in contrast, often has more abstract results and a fluid sequence of activities.

Focusing on the result and benefit to the organization can help achieve clarity here. If some concrete and measurable metrics can be established that the change is intended to meet, the success of the transformation can be assessed through these metrics.

However, there is what Doug Hubbard calls the problem of "measurement inversion."[13] Many businesses, projects included, tend to measure what is easy. They often do not measure what provides the most significant information value for their decision making. To assess success, they measure the cost against the budget of a transformation and the progress against a deadline. Yet the most considerable value lies in the benefits, which rarely get measured.

An example of better metrics in action is defining a change in behavior and its intended benefit. For example, you specify that in the future, after the system has gone live, your end users will engage with the new processes. As a result, you expect sales to increase by 5%.

This approach is inspired by the Lean Start-Up Model[14] by Eric Ries, an American entrepreneur and author: Make assumptions about what would benefit your users, take a leap of faith in the assumptions, build something, test it with users in the market, learn, and improve iteratively.

The goals to be achieved then become:

1. The system successfully goes live: first as a prototype, then an alpha version, an invitation-only beta version, a public beta version, and finally, the final version.
2. End users both use and engage with the system, with the goal of understanding the new systems and processes, which is demonstrated by their successful use, the quality of the data entered, and user satisfaction.
3. Sales have increased by the expected amount as user numbers grow.

Another approach is what we call governance by prototypes. As we discussed earlier in this chapter, in designing your system, you have identified up to five specific, low-level processes and functions that the system will perform. Having a small set of core process, in combination with awareness of the intended benefits, allows you to measure the progress of the prototype.

As the prototype is developed and iterated on, you can measure its performance in many of the intended functions. Then, while testing it – potentially as part of training based on the prototype build – you can measure how well it provides the intended benefit.

The second model, more closely inspired by the design thinking approach, typically is more suited to situations where the organization is risk averse – you do not want to launch too early – or in situations where you cannot implement the technology in many little iterations, such as where a complex network of legacy software might be disrupted in surprising ways.

Many software companies have adopted the old 3M idea of 15% innovation time; some companies even allow 20%. However, a senior engineer and team leader at a large software company explained to us that 20% of innovation time is not set in stone.

1. The line manager must agree that you can spend time on the idea.
2. Some mission-critical products are out of bounds. Changes to core products go through monthlong rigorous governance before the code is committed.
3. You can make changes only if you can roll them back.
4. Failure is fantastic, and there is no blame for failing with an idea, but a forensic analysis must happen afterward. You cannot just crumple your notes, throw them in the bin, and start something new.

Working with change leaders, we found that it is beneficial to develop your approach to change by asking two questions:

1. Are the intended outcomes, benefits, and results clearly defined (yes/no)?
2. Is the sequence of activities we need to do clearly defined (yes/no)?

These questions provide you with a typology of change (Table 5.3) that was first described by Eddie Obeng[15] and is based on research by Rodney Turner and Robert Cochrane.[16]

If you answer yes to both questions, you are in the territory of the so-called paint-by-numbers project. You can define your work breakdown structure, define milestones, draw up Gantt charts, and so on. The critical leadership and governance challenge is tracking milestone completion, keeping up with slippages, and managing workstream interdependencies.

TABLE 5.3 Four types of change projects.

	Process/sequence clear	Process/sequence unclear
Outcome clear	Paint by numbers – know what to do, know what the result will be.	Quest – Try stuff in parallel, see what works.
Outcome unclear	Making a movie – the process is clear, it's the same every time. Result might be different, not clear till finished.	Walking in the fog – primary goal is to get out into where either process or outcome or both are clear.

If your answer is no to both questions, your project will be like walking in the fog. It would be best to get out of the fog. If you are walking in the mountains and fog descends, a lovely Sunday afternoon turns life-threatening.

As the leader, you need to get your team to hold hands (or a safety line) and define a walking direction by identifying a beacon most likely to get you out of the fog. When you get to the beacon, you must ensure that the whole team is still together and aligned. Then, as the leader, you pick the next beacon. The critical governance challenge in projects of this type is to decide whether the project should be canceled because it will always stay in the fog.

If your project has a clear outcome but a completely unclear sequence of activities, we call the project type a quest. Since no one knows the best sequence of activities, what we need to do is explore different approaches to delivering the outcomes – not sequentially – that would be too slow – but in parallel.

The metaphor is borrowed from King Arthur, who sent his knights in shining armor on a quest for the Holy Grail. Instead of letting each try and fail in turn, he sent them all out in different directions at once to try their approaches.

However, in projects, we do not always have the resources to spin up three separate projects tasked with solving an issue and then reporting back a year later. Instead, the idea of the quest is most often used by setting up short and sharp task forces. Hackathons are also great examples. For example, a hackathon could have the theme of project data. An organization we worked with issued an open invitation to anyone interested in helping. Mostly students responded to the call. The organization shared real-world data sets about their project, and hackathon participants had one weekend to come up with creative prototypes that used the data. Some teams tried AI for better forecasts, other teams worked on visualizations. At the end of the hackathon, a jury selected the best ideas and handed out a small price.

The critical leadership and governance challenge is the cost of this approach – these projects burn cash! Thus, leaders need to monitor resources and close down unpromising workstreams, combining the best ideas from different workstreams.

Finally, if your project has a clear sequence of activities but lacks clarity on the outcome, you are in the space of design thinking, creativity, and innovation. These projects are like making movies. Movies are all made with the exact same process: There is an idea, someone writes a treatment, a script is developed, actors are hired, locations are scouted, filming takes place, editing occurs, and, finally, there is a marketing machine and a release date.

All movies – flops and blockbusters alike – use a well-established process. In technology transformations, this process might be the discovery and design process, the diamond innovation model, or the SCRUM process.

The key leadership challenge in these projects is to balance the divergence and convergence process. Divergence involves developing crazy ideas, while convergence involves putting together a workable prototype to get feedback.

In short, this framework, known as the fog-quest-movie-PbN framework, is useful for recognizing that you can create a milestone-based approach for your change only if you are in paint-by-numbers territory. Admittedly, you can always define milestones, but they are useless at best and a distraction at worst in fog, quest, or movie projects.

This framework also highlights the dynamics of change. Transformations often start in the fog and then mature into quests, movies, or paint-by-number projects. You must understand the leadership and governance challenge and create an appropriate approach.

Ultimately, the keys to defining the approach to a transformation are awareness, flexibility, and balance. No two businesses are the same, and neither will there be two digital transformations. This means that you, as the person in charge of the transformation, must ensure that the approach fits the needs and demands of both the permanent organization and the project itself.

Doing this requires that you spend time specifically on analyzing the organization and selecting the approach that will operate best for the transformation at hand. It also requires designing an approach to measuring and managing progress that is good for now. However, a balance between planning and action needs to be maintained. While it is true that leaping into the project without taking time to look will cause problems, spending too much time agonizing over the precisely perfect approach will also cause issues and delays.

Feel free to adjust your approach if you realize that you need to adapt to the unexpected once you have begun your transformation.

Lever #3: Early Involvement of Users

A common but ultimately ineffective approach to transformation is what a colleague once memorably referred to as submarine-style implementation. This style of implementation takes all the required requirements and resources down to the bottom of the ocean – where nobody can see or hear anything about what is going on – and then surfaces eight months later with the system.

In such cases, the first-time end users encounter the new systems and processes is when the project is in a "finished" state. Thus, any user feedback can happen only at around the point when the systems are intended to go live. Imagine the chaos if the project surfaces from the inky depths and doesn't do what it needs to!

While most organizations do not tend to shut out users entirely, it is true that a traditional top-down approach does not make the most of end users. The waterfall approach, in which steps cascade downward, studies and gathers requirements at the start – hopefully in part by interviewing users.

After this, users are absent for long periods until testing happens at the end, sometimes years later. This is like the Queensland Health payroll system we mentioned in the introduction, which went live and immediately produced 35,000 payroll mistakes.

Modern thinking and mindsets are starting to challenge this traditional approach, however. In the 1990s, new ideas emerged that brought us continuous testing and the use of mock-ups.[1] These days, the agile community is leading the charge. A feature of the agile methodology focuses on getting users involved and providing feedback early on and regularly. As this new feedback is collected, it is used to adjust and optimize the transformation in motion rather than at a specific stage toward the end of a project in which feedback is gathered and implemented.

As one of our interviewees succinctly put it:

The business implications of implementing new systems and processes were greatly underestimated. [In this case, all systems related
to customer relationship management and sales will transform in
major ways.] There were (and to some extent are still) many frustrations with the result, largely due to not consulting key users and
change agents but designing and implementing [systems and pro-
cesses] in our headquarters.

And another interviewee shared a horrible experience:

First, when they got this new application, the clinicians didn't think it
was usable. You couldn't figure the app out – and it all ended badly.
Then serious mistakes also happened, which meant some patients
were wrongly medicated, and the project had to be closed. My old
colleagues at the hospitals were furious with the project. I was also
completely done myself when I was done with the project.

> [Kim] In one transformation that can be considered an example of an
> alternative to the waterfall approach, we created a *waterwheel*. In the
> waterfall approach, direction flows from the top of the organization
> downward to the bottom. In a waterwheel approach, the direction and
> leadership flowing down from the top are informed by feedback and
> input carried up from the grassroots of the organization.
>
> The waterwheel idea emphasized and achieved the goal of getting
> top management into a listening mode by defining the flow of informa-
> tion that would spin the wheel.

The rising popularity of agile methodologies was, in fact, a motivating
force behind our research. We analyzed organizational change management
frameworks and found that most were based on the traditional top-down
waterfall approach. Yet you will be hard-pressed to find a technology change
approach that uses the classic waterfall without any components of the agile
toolkit. We decided to gather data to support our philosophy that involving
users as early and as much as possible is good.

Surprisingly, Some Digital Transformations Did Not Involve Users

There are several reasons why users might be overlooked or deliberately excluded in a project. One might be a desire by the digital transformation or by its leader to avoid involving users at a point in the project where things are still uncertain. Not all users react well to high uncertainty – involving such users too early in the project when things have not been finalized yet might damage their trust in the result, an attitude that might spread throughout the organization.

In 7 of the 155 transformations we researched, we found that – surprisingly – the project managers admitted to not having engaged with the end users. The two key reasons given were that the software was intended to be used out of the box without any alterations – with no customization required; it was assumed user feedback was unnecessary – and that there had simply been no time to engage with end users.

In all seven of those transformations, leaders quickly realized their mistake. Lack of user involvement early on led to delays in the project later. All seven were forced to try to make up for this mistake with later testing activities. In hindsight, all interviewees regretted not involving the users.

Interestingly, when we investigated one digital transformation in an African bank, the project leader reflected that time pressures are always high in their organization and, historically, projects used to skip user involvement and testing. As a result, organizational policy now mandated involvement of users early and throughout, including testing. Guess what: Subsequent transformations went exceptionally well in understanding, meeting, and managing user expectations.

Another reason for not involving users might be that end users end up in a blind spot when the transformation is being planned. In a business-to-business transformations, for example, the transformation might introduce changes to a customer who is part of a different organization, and the closest you can get to the actual customer is the salespeople.

Digital transformations often do not benefit end users; rather, they might improve a process for the organization or for customers. Implementations for enterprise resource planning systems, for example, might improve data quality or team coordination for management.

Since the purpose is not to benefit the user, the focus is on how well the new technology fulfills its purpose, for example a cost reduction – not the user's perspective or experience. Imagine your smartphone; apps designed to maintain the phone will not be particularly attractive or intuitive. Apps targeting users, like Snapchat, Candy Crush, Facebook, or LinkedIn, will, however, be designed specifically with users in mind.

Case Study: Who Are the Benefits For?

[Kim] I was working on a digital transformation in finance in a company that was also working on a second, completely different transformation with very different priorities. The finance transformation was intended to mostly benefit the organization, not the end users; it was going to optimize IT security and data quality and standardize technology across the organization. These definitely don't sound like interesting and "sexy" things.

The second transformation, in contrast, was far more extraordinary (particularly for end users). It was intended to improve the end user experience in the workplace. The transformation involved investigating user needs and solving pain points with impressive apps and other creative solutions.

The fundamentally different ways of thinking about change and designing a solution sometimes result in a confusing tonal whiplash for users. The user experience project promises to do anything users want – dream it, and it'll happen. The focus is 100% on the user. Our finance transformation, however, isn't really for them; we are constrained by the organization's needs, regulations, auditors, and so on. By comparison, it is far more complicated for us to promise to solve all of the user's problems.

As discussed in previous chapters, the organization's and users' pain points often are not directly aligned. Engaging users will not discover how well the system addresses the organization's pain points. However, users must adopt a new system or process to realize the organizational benefits. Thus, the challenge for digital transformations is balancing the users' and organization's requirements and finding solutions that simultaneously address both.

Indeed, the case study rings true. In a couple of case examples, a project that was initially thought of as a software upgrade turned into a true transformation, as most processes had to change. We also learned about cybersecurity projects where only halfway through the project was it recognized that no significant security gains would be made without users' behavioral changes.

Another common concern we raised in our interviews is that if you ask users for their opinions, they demand things, leading to scope creep, delays, and extra costs. One participant said, "The system specification was already chrome-plated; had we not curtailed the end user involvement, we would have gold-plated the whole thing."

A final but important reason users were left out was that while nearly everyone understands that user involvement is a great idea, some find the idea hard to implement. Time pressures and access to the right end users complicate successful user involvement.

Projects don't benefit from involving just anyone, and the people who can contribute the most value are often the busiest. Many projects cited multiple transformations going on at the same time, and expert resources were too stretched to work meaningfully with all the transformations and changes going on.

In projects that struggled to bring in users, staff turnover often exacerbated the shortage of expert resources throughout the project. User turnover led to continual loss of knowledge and increased the time required to bring them up to speed with the transformation. Some transformations can take more than three years, and often, especially in the public sector, most experts change roles every two years. So, recruiting and keeping experts is one of the most significant barriers to user involvement.

Case Study: Failure of the National Health Service IT Programme

[Alex] The National Programme for IT in the UK National Health Service – also called NPfIT – is often recognized as the mother of all failed technology transformations. The NHS suffered a spectacular failure in its attempts to implement a digital transformation due to a lack of user feedback. However, it did not fail quite how you would expect projects to fail.

The NHS wanted to optimize its data collection and IT systems for managing information about patients and their diagnoses – what the industry calls electronic medical records. To do this, the NHS created a data entry mechanism with detailed disease classifications for diagnosis.

The problem was that those in charge of planning the project misidentified the end user. They thought that the system's users would be doctors. The assumption was that if it was the doctor who performed the diagnosis, then it would be the doctor who entered the data. The system was designed accordingly – you needed a medical degree to enter data correctly.

Project planners did not realize or understand that, in a hospital setting, doctors typically don't do data entry. Nurses were the ones doing the data entry, and, therefore, nurses were the actual end users of the

(continued)

(continued)

system. Nurses did not have the same degree of training – they were unaware of the exact fine details and nuances that a doctor would know.

Why did the transformation fail to engage nurses properly? In many clinical settings, doctors are the authority figures. They are loud voices and have much more power than nurses, which might have contributed to nurses being overlooked.

The data entry system was designed assuming the end user has a doctor's technical medical knowledge, which led to problems. Nurses, struggling with a system not designed for them, made data entry errors, which corrupted and made the data collected hard to use. Ultimately, the system could not meet NHS needs because it had been designed without considering the end user experience and feedback.

If the end user perspective had been considered earlier, the failure could have been avoided. Developers would have received feedback from doctors that nurses would be using the system. Then developers could have engaged with nurses to design and test a disease classification scheme that fulfilled the needs of the NHS and its nurses.

However, as sociologists Geoffrey C. Bowker and Susan Leigh Star[2] have discovered, technology is frozen organizational and political discourse. In other words, due to power relations within organizations, like the ones between doctors and nurses, end users might need a voice. Any transformation that challenges the power structure needs to be prepared to work on organizational politics to be successful.

But What If Users Have Ideas?

Some of the transformations we studied spoke to the fear that when you ask users what they want, you will receive requests that invariably add cost and delay to the project. However, as we found out, this is no reason to avoid engaging end users; it only wastes money if the transformation says yes to every idea. Instead, leaders need to learn how to say no.

Our colleague Alan South, former managing director of IDEO Europe and chief innovation officer at Solarcentury, highlights the challenge of saying no in his disciplined corporate entrepreneurship model (Figure 6.1).

The first step of the innovation funnel, insights, and opportunities is rarely the problem. Organizations' users are typically full of good ideas.

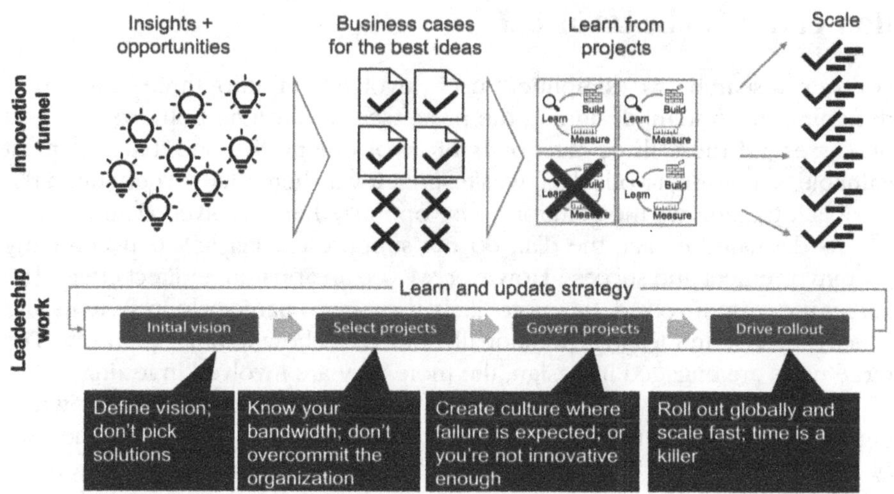

FIGURE 6.1 The model of disciplined entrepreneurship.

Leadership's task is to provide focus by setting a vision and then letting the users generate ideas.

The second step of the funnel is to create and select business cases for the best ideas. The key challenge for leaders is to regulate the organization's bandwidth. There are always more good and profitable ideas than can be implemented.

The third step is to pilot innovations. Start with small prototypes: build, measure, learn, and then iterate for improvements. The key leadership challenge is to make the failure of these projects acceptable. Indeed, Alan explains that if all projects succeed, the organization misses an opportunity, and the pilot projects need more ambition.

The fourth step is to roll out the pilots at scale and pace. The leadership challenge here is to make the scaling happen.

Like the challenge of saying no to users and stakeholders with good ideas, the key to disciplined entrepreneurship is killing good and bad ideas, and then implementing the ideas in pilot projects and rolling out the successful projects. Saying no to ideas needs to be done fairly and justly. What are required are rules[3] that define when an idea should not go ahead. Thus, before engaging with users to generate ideas, transformations need to have a clear set of tests that must be applied to advance an idea to the next stage or kill it off.

How Can Users Be Involved?

For our research, we simplified user involvement into three categories: designing the system, designing the processes, and testing both systems and processes. Of these three categories of involvement, the one that was most valuable, according to our data, was testing. It was here that we generated the feedback that allows the solution to be optimized and evolved (Figure 6.2).

As discussed earlier, the data do not support a direct link between early user involvement and success. However, we see an apparent indirect effect. The earlier users are involved, the more likely they are to participate in systems and process design and testing. Additionally, our data show another pathway: The more users are engaged in design, the more they are involved in testing.

If users are involved early, we tend to test early. In the model shown in Figure 6.2, we measured the point when users were first involved. The start of the transformation got a value of 1 and the end of the transformation got a value of 10. The negative association shown in the chart means that the

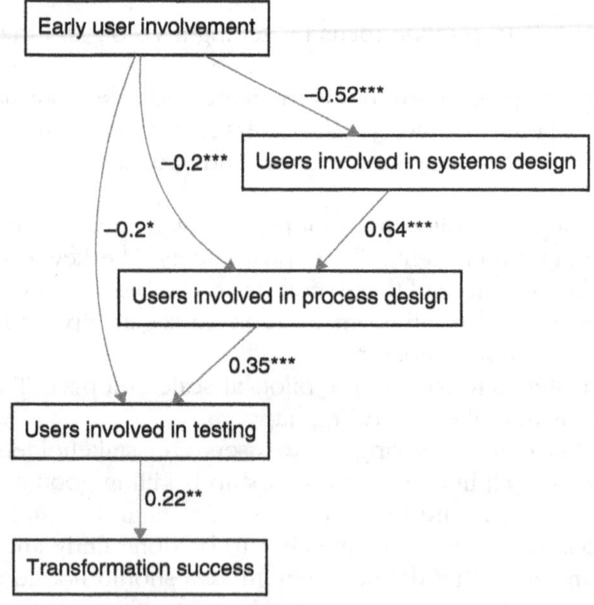

FIGURE 6.2 Model of the indirect effects of early user involvement associated with transformation success. The figure shows only coefficients of statistically significant paths. Stars indicate statistical significance: *** $p \leq 0.001$, ** $p \leq 0.01$, * $p \leq 0.05$.

earlier users are involved, the earlier and the more regularly we test. This, in turn, increases the chances of success.

We find only an indirect link between transformation success and engaging users to help design the system and processes. We found that user involvement in testing directly impacts success. However, according to our data, the more users engage with the design of systems and processes, the more likely they are to test things and provide feedback.

However, involving users in the design does not improve the chances of success directly or indirectly above and beyond their crucial role in testing. In short, the more users are involved in testing, the more successful the transformation will likely be; the earlier we start testing, the better.

Involving users in design can be a potentially dangerous trap. Such user involvement can lead to a false confidence that because the users helped to design the systems and processes, the systems and processes will meet the end users' needs. This is not automatically true. Even if the users designed everything, the systems should be tested to ensure they work as intended.

Imagine a child being asked to design their dream home. Even if you can give them everything they dreamed of, they might still not appreciate the result. Like the famous story of the Ford Edsel, the hallmark of all market failures was designed through market research. Indeed, a car designed according to what the market said it wanted would be perfect; however, it was a total flop.

While any child will know exactly what they want and what they do not, the finished house might be different from what they need. For example, a child might have detailed ideas on how to design their perfect playroom but see no reason to consider plumbing, wiring, or rooms like the kitchen or toilet!

The same thing happened again in the construction world. Extensive stretches of Dubai are filled with beautiful skyscrapers, yet because their designers focused on the glitz and glamor over the practicalities, they never built a sewage system. To this day, big trucks still have to empty septic tanks in the basements of these buildings.

Only by seeing and experiencing the solution in person can they see how well the separate aspects of their design interact and function together.

Famously, the challenge of identifying a complete set of user requirements is encapsulated in the Kano model of user satisfaction with a product, system, or service (Figure 6.3).[4] The Kano model conveys a critical message. When you ask users for their requirements, they only tell you about revealed quality characteristics. Revealed characteristics are those where the better the features work, the more satisfied the user will be with the quality, and the less the features work, the greater the dissatisfaction.

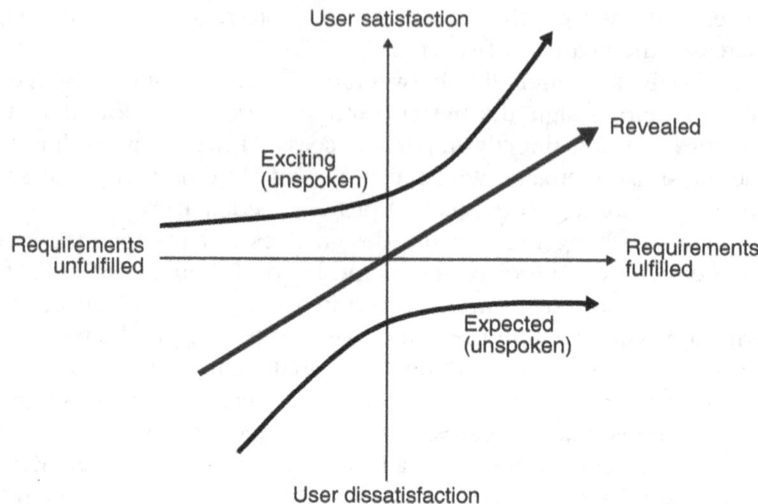

FIGURE 6.3 The Kano model of spoken and unspoken user requirements.

The big drawback of user interviews is that they cannot tell you about features that would wow them, create delight, and excite them. If these features do not work, they will not generate any dissatisfaction. Finally, users typically cannot tell you about basic expected features. Features are just expected to work, adding nothing to the users' satisfaction but creating dissatisfaction if they do not work. And this is why prototyping is such a powerful way to involve users.

Another benefit to prototyping is how it naturally builds trust and interest in the new systems. As end users practice with and explore the benefits of the prototype, they discover how the new systems benefit them. Doing this allows them to share their perspectives and views, allowing you to create positive testimonials to share and informally pass their experiences onto their colleagues (Figure 6.3).

Testing is the top priority for user involvement. This testing needs to happen as early as possible. The earlier this testing begins, the more user involvement there will be, maximizing the benefit of the transformation.

Stages of Testing

We mentioned earlier that uncertainty is an issue with testing earlier in a transformation. Until a certain point in the project's life cycle, things will be more up in the air. This reality should not stop testing from happening – in fact, it is far easier to adapt and evolve the solution with feedback at this stage. However, it is crucial to ensure that testers are aware of the solution's development stage.

Testers will interact with a prototype while still in development. To avoid false hopes or fears, they need to know what stage of development that prototype represents. Otherwise, you risk users becoming confused, believing that a 30% completed prototype is the finished product and beginning to panic that it cannot work.

Conversely, we have seen projects where senior managers get impatient, look at a prototype, and push for immediate release into productivity. Because we manage satisfaction, it is vital to remember that *Satisfaction = Reality ÷ Expectation*. Accordingly, expectation management is as important as the delivery of helpful change.

Prototyping

As with training, the key to effectively testing through prototypes is to provide an experience of the processes in action. For a data entry system, doing this is often simple enough. It is easy enough to replicate and simulate the workflow on a computer, though it is important to account for "real-world processes," such as needing to print documentation or interact with others.

We found that it is helpful to remember that human-centered design is more than designing an interface or a user experience – the focus is creating a user's long-term relationship. To do so, prototypes do not have to be a version of a new system. Storyboards, maps, and role-plays make great prototypes in the early stages.

However, more complicated systems might require more elaborate forms of prototyping. In Chapter 9, we look at various creative ways of simulating systems for training.

Case Study: Simulating Construction Projects in Minecraft

[Alex] Using computer programs to simulate in 3D what a process or system would look like can be a compelling application of modern technology. Virtual reality (VR) technology is a fantastic application – house-hunting websites apply this to allow virtual tours of apartments without needing to leave your home, for example.

My favorite example of this method in action came from a construction company using simulation to optimize working practices and coordination on the site. In this case, the purpose was not to change the organization but to build a motorway in Cambridgeshire. However, the

(continued)

(continued)

company wanted to do this more efficiently. To do so, it made a digital model of the construction site and the surrounding towns, villages, roads, and countryside.

A key challenge for the project was constructing a bridge and a major junction with another motorway. Typically, such a significant construction effort would take eight weeks to demolish the old bridge and build a new one. Over that time, the company would need to close the road every weekend for the entire weekend. Simulating the work, allowing the company to visualize how the various processes interacted, revolutionized how the different trades worked together – the whole bridge replacement was completed in a single weekend.

What might surprise people is how the project also used its digital model to engage with stakeholders – it did it in the video game Minecraft. For those unfamiliar with it, Minecraft is a video game that allows people to build elaborate constructions or virtually explore what others have made by visiting other people's online servers.

One way the Minecraft version of the project was used was by applying this project to fulfilling a company value of encouraging children's interest in engineering. Staff members went into local schools and allowed children to play with the model on their Minecraft server. This activity worked incredibly well. Children loved the opportunity to find their own houses in the model – then virtually blow them up (a common but reversible activity of those visiting a new Minecraft server).

The ability to present construction projects in the local area is not only an effective way to prototype and simulate the project itself, it is also a fantastic means to reach out to the community impacted by the work and create positive sentiment. In addition, the Minecraft version showed construction progress in real time.

If nothing else, I am sure that parents would be relieved to hear that, while their child might have blown up their house, the construction company has no such intention in real life!

Who Should Be Involved in the Testing?

As we have said, early-stage prototypes and the alpha stages of testing very rarely reflect the intended end goal of the transformation. In addition, while users are aware of the pain points facing them specifically, they might not always have the vision to see the technology's potential or the understanding of the organization's needs and pain points required to make their feedback truly relevant in the alpha stages of testing.

You need end users involved in the early stages of testing to think outside their box and be knowledgeable and experienced in the organization. An example is an apocryphal quote attributed to Henry Ford regarding car design: "If I had asked people what they had wanted, they would have asked me for faster horses."

People are aware of the problems they face – horses were not fast enough – but the average person might not have the perspective to begin designing an effective solution. Such a person would have seen the early prototypes of a car and complained that it could not possibly replace a horse – feedback that would not help design a better car.

Even if Henry Ford never said those words, it is a brief reminder that user interviews, written use cases, and user stories rarely surface the requirements that excite users and the expected requirements.

How can you innovate within the typical constraints of risk-averse organizations? The answer lies in prototyping. Every organization is full of good ideas – creativity is rarely the problem in innovation. The critical issue is to be disciplined. The diamond model, from the Design Thinking community, offers a good guide.[5]

Visually, the model shows an equal balance between the divergent phase of the project – where you create lots of good ideas – and the convergent phase – where your team needs to make choices to develop a prototype that users then test. Based on their feedback and ideas, you start the next iteration of the diamond. In this model, we highlighted the importance of turning the corner. As the project leader, you need to get the timing right (Figure 6.4).

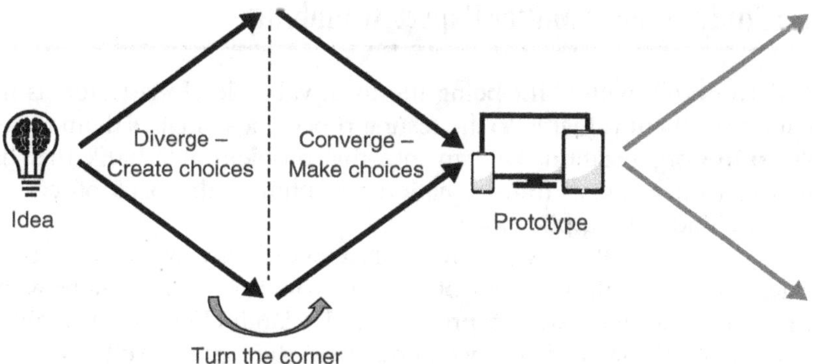

FIGURE 6.4 The diamond model of human-centric prototyping.

We worked with German computer engineers on one of our projects. The project tried to develop innovative products, and after several new product development meetings, we noticed a pattern.

In a two-week innovation sprint, the engineers would attend our kick-off meeting. However, if they had not identified and nailed down a solution by the end of the meeting, they would be profoundly uneasy and see the meeting as a failure. They engaged in divergent thinking for a maximum of the first half hour of the meeting, and for the rest of the sprint, they would try to make it perfect – a lost opportunity to be innovative.

In contrast, we worked on some highly creative marketing projects. This time, we were not with computer engineers but with experts from an advertising agency. They had the opposite problem from the engineers. We discussed the brief. Two weeks later, they came back to pitch a campaign, and it was always a hot mess of ideas.

The team had so much divergent thinking that they got around to converging their ideas into a cohesive campaign only when they sat in the taxi to drive to our offices. Again, this is a lost opportunity. For some strange reason, they always pitched us to buy a branded blimp – they were also not great at listening when we, as the client, actually made choices for them and always turned down the blimp idea. The blimp quickly became a running joke in our team every time we walked into the room to meet agency staff.

As a project leader, it is vital to manage the team to turn the corner to balance innovation and get a prototype ready to test with users. Depending on your situation, you might have to manage reluctant engineers to devote more time to developing ideas, or you might need to manage your hypercreative team to make choices earlier. Then you need the organization's subject matter experts (SMEs) to help test from the start.

Case Study: Subject Matter Expert Availability

[Alex] The catch with SMEs being the most valuable alpha testers is that what makes them valuable to the testing process also makes them invaluable to the organization. We ran into this problem at a bank that had embarked on a digital transformation to optimize the back-office processes behind loan applications.

In that office, there were over 100 workers. Involving all of them, particularly at the alpha stages of testing, would not work. There would be far too much feedback to process, and a large chunk of it might be coming from those who did not understand the system well enough to provide input that addressed the bank's pain points. After all, processes work best when they flow, and the typical stoppage is the handover between departments. You need experts who know about their work and a little about the work in other departments through which it flows.

Through interviews, it soon became clear who we needed to talk to. Only five people had the expertise we were after. They knew the system perfectly and had the most experience in how the bank operated – including the processes behind analyzing the risks of loans and accepting or rejecting applications accordingly. As a result, only these five were trusted with the most complicated and high-risk accounts.

The office regarded them as wise sages. Their knowledge and history of mastering every aspect of the processes made them a valuable resource to the organization. We needed their input for testing.

However, they were the most complicated people to schedule time with to *do* the testing. What made them so valuable to us meant they were irreplaceable – nobody else could do their work. If we had needed to take anybody else, one of the "sages" could have covered what might have taken anyone else a day within an hour. Only these experts were capable of covering their role, though.

This meant that scheduling even one of them for testing purposes required much work, convincing senior management to part with them.

Case Study: Scheduling Subject Matter Experts

[Alex] A leader we interviewed shared his experience struggling with this difficulty in scheduling experts for testing. This transformation – installing new wealth management systems for a multinational bank with over 60,000 employees – initially did what most projects would do and asked for a part-time allocation of an expert, for example, requesting 0.1 full-time equivalent (FTE) from the risk department. This ended badly for them.

Germany was chosen as the pilot. The technical solution for the pilot was based on analyzing the organization's detailed process maps and documentation. Based on these data, they determined how to improve these processes and integrated these changes into the system.

Disaster ensued when the first release hit user testing. The documented processes did not reflect how the end users worked in reality. The resulting chaos was expensive, and the consequent distrust of

(continued)

(continued)

management and the new systems bred a lot of resistance in their German user community.

So, they had to go back to the drawing board. Having been burnt once already, they realized they had to find out how things worked on the ground. Once they started looking for them, the project lead found it easy to discover the SMEs. For once, they were the loudest voices pointing out all the different ways in which the pilot was an unmitigated disaster.

If you ask multiple groups of employees to tell them who they go to for help or support, you will notice that the same few names will eventually keep coming up – those are who you need to schedule for testing. As with the previous case study, the struggle was scheduling testing time.

In this case, the project management team produced a remarkably detailed timeline of the next phase, outlining important dates to receive feedback. As their experts' time was so valuable, they had to spend two months coordinating the logistics of scheduling testing time – sometimes over a year in advance!

A typical timeline would be that a prototype would be ready by this Wednesday in January, and they would need two full days for feedback from the SMEs for the rest of the week. The project started to turn around thanks to the SMEs' scheduled and structured input.

The next challenge they discovered was that these SMEs could not sign off on processes changes. Often they needed more authority. The project started to create a list of all business decisions that needed to be made and which person or committee would be required to make those.

Together, these two changes to how the project managed the change proved successful. Enabling the SMEs to take control of their schedules and deliver accordingly eliminated all further delays. The combination of detailed SME resource planning and the "open decisions" lists was replicated in the much smoother rollouts for the remaining countries, delivering on budget and on time.

This approach had such an impact that the bank has used it to schedule SMEs as a blueprint for all of its complex projects.

When to Move from SME Testing into General User Testing

Moving from alpha testing with experts to beta testing with a broader pool of users is a process that we can't offer precise advice or data beyond "When it feels right." What we *can* advise is what the right feeling looks like.

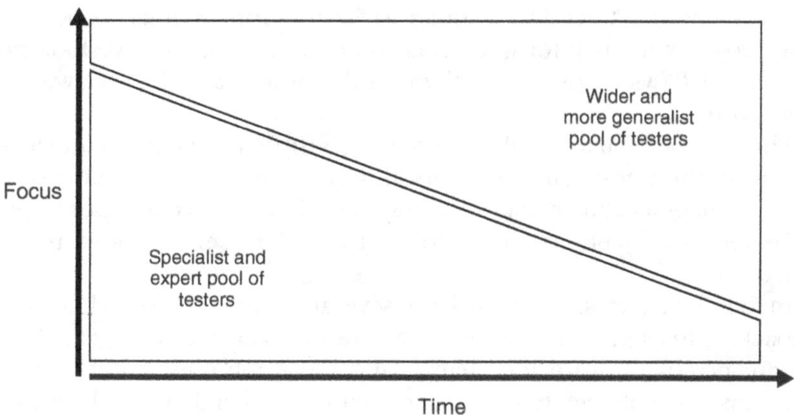

FIGURE 6.5 The model of balancing effort to test technology change.

Testing with prototypes will always be a cyclical process – you will provide a prototype to your testers, they will test it and provide feedback, and you will go away and implement this feedback for the next build. The point at which beta testing should start is when the alpha testing feedback starts drying up.

At this point, you need to expand the pool of testers. The prototype model will likely fit the organization's needs as well as possible at this stage. What needs to happen is to interact with a wider pool of users – feedback generated here will further refine and optimize the prototype.

It will also be possible to start considering designing the training program – use your SMEs to help train the expanded pool on the prototype.

These waves of expansion may be repeated, expanding to a broader range of users repeatedly as feedback from the previous testing stage begins to dry up (Figure 6.5).

Seeking Criticism

People dislike change, so it will be inevitable that any transformation will gather its critics and fans. If the goal of the transformation is not to make the users happy, then dissatisfaction is inevitable. The question becomes, how do we manage these people who hate the changes?

In *Dune*, a science fiction series by Frank Herbert, a political organization famous for complex and ambitious schemes takes a seemingly bizarre approach to project management by putting the project's greatest critic in charge.

While you don't need to go quite so far, this approach has benefits. Fans of the project will push for it to succeed and might miss or overlook potential issues or flaws. Those not in favor of the project are already aware of its flaws and risks.

This makes them a valuable source of constructive feedback and a useful measure of the transformation's appeal. If you can optimize and evolve the project to meet its aims while satisfying their doubts or concerns, the project will be far more likely to appeal to your broader user base and, therefore, to succeed.

In our interviews, we heard on several occasions that when seeking feedback in testing, you should make sure that you include a mix of those who are positive toward the change and those who are hostile toward it. Doing this prevents creating an accidental echo chamber in which passion for the technology leads to it creeping off-mission.

You need someone whose role is to challenge the changes and ensure that they genuinely address the pain points the transformation intends to fix. In our study, the projects that did not do this in the first place encountered issues later when scope changes became more complex and time-consuming to implement.

What We Learned from Our Research

By involving users from the start, you can benefit from their experience and perspective on the technology and the transformation. Of course, you need to structure and manage their involvement to ensure that the users you include can provide the feedback that will be most valuable at that stage of the testing process.

This means that you need to identify your most valuable SMEs for the early stages of testing. The most significant challenge is that the value of these SMEs means that their availability and involvement with the project need to be scheduled as early as possible – if not, often it is difficult to spare them from their other commitments.

Successfully involving users in the testing process also allows you to start informing and managing other aspects of the transformation, such as optimizing and planning training, which we look at more in Chapter 9.

CHAPTER 7

Lever #4: Management Ownership

When discussing management and managers during our investigations, we split them into three levels: top, middle, and frontline managers.[1] While these terms are familiar to most, it might be helpful to define them as they were used in our research.

- Top management: The highest level of leadership, including the C-suite executives. Generally in charge of directing and organizing the company and making the big decisions.
- Middle management: The layers of leadership below the chief executive level and above the frontline managers. They are in charge of helping to realize top management's goals and directives by making sure that information and resources are available and by coordinating team leaders.
- Frontline management: The direct leaders and line managers of employees. They are the first line of contact and communication between the employees and the organization.

As Chapter 1 describes, managing organizational change is often treated as an afterthought when planning the transformation strategy. A team of internal and external change experts might be tasked with a workstream and left to get on with it; this is not enough.

It is easy for an organization's managers to assume that they do not need to involve themselves, leaving change management to the project manager and the change experts. Senior managers have all encountered this fire-and-forget mentality.

The data show clearly that when management – at all levels – increases their engagement with a transformation, the chances of success increase. The home-team advantage of an organization's management becoming involved cannot be ignored.

Why? Our research question explores the complex interface between the temporary organization[2] – the project – and the permanent organization – the transformation owner.

The temporary organization and its leaders are on one side of the transformation, and the permanent organization and its leaders are on the other.

The project leadership team will be there only until the project closes down. Typically the team is disbanded after a short post-launch support phase. Once the project is closed, they move on to the next project and the subsequent development cycle.[3]

A key fault line in transformations appears when the temporary organization delivers a new system and then hands it over to the permanent organization, which realizes the project's benefits. In many projects, this handover is when things go wrong. The responsibilities of realizing the benefits are unclear, and monitoring and controlling stop and holding leaders accountable stops.

In one of the cases we studied, we heard of a system where, after the project went live, the core project leadership team stayed on while most team members left.

In this organization, each project reported to a steering committee that brought together senior leaders from all involved units of the business. The project leaders, including the project management office responsible for compiling reports, continued to report back for another two reporting cycles – six months – about the benefits realized after going live.

Continuing the steering committee meetings ensured accountability and problem-solving, especially where achieving benefits required collaboration between siloes of the organization.

Successfully creating and implementing a project does not mean that the transformation is realizing its intended benefits to the permanent organization. The people in charge of realizing the benefits of the transformation are not the project team – they're the management teams and business units of the permanent organization.

The key to ensuring that the permanent organization enjoys the benefits of the transformation is for top, middle, and frontline managers to own the transformation.

As for what that engagement looks like, we have identified three archetypal ways management engages with a transformation: support, promote, and own. The precise nature of each action varies according to the manager's seniority, but they are all relevant and impactful at every level of seniority.

Support

For managers, supporting a transformation usually is about making resources available. Managers understand that there is a benefit to be gained for the company and is willing to provide what is at their disposal to make it happen. The resources provided depend on the managers' seniority but include time, funding, workforce, expertise, and others. We consider this the lowest level of engagement because often it involves just participating in the investment decision to approve funding.

Promote

Promotion of a transformation ties into communicating about the project to others. When managers promote the transformation, they speak positively about it – perhaps by sharing its benefits with stakeholders or end users (depending on the managers' seniority). The result of successful promotion is generally increased awareness of the transformation in the organization and a positive attitude toward it.

Own

When managers own a transformation, they have emotionally and logically bought into the project, are engaged in it, and actively involve themselves with it. Doing this includes taking control of the transformation – they make themselves responsible for running the project and are directly invested in and accountable for delivering the results. Ultimately, these managers view it as *their* project. We consider this to be the highest level of management engagement.

What Data Do We Have?

In our research, we quickly noticed a clear trend in our data on how management engages with transformations. We measured the engagement on a scale from 1 to 10. In the data, top management (C-suite) was universally more involved in every way; frontline management, in contrast, had the most minor engagement.[4] Additionally, support was the most common type of engagement, and ownership was the least (Figure 7.1).[5]

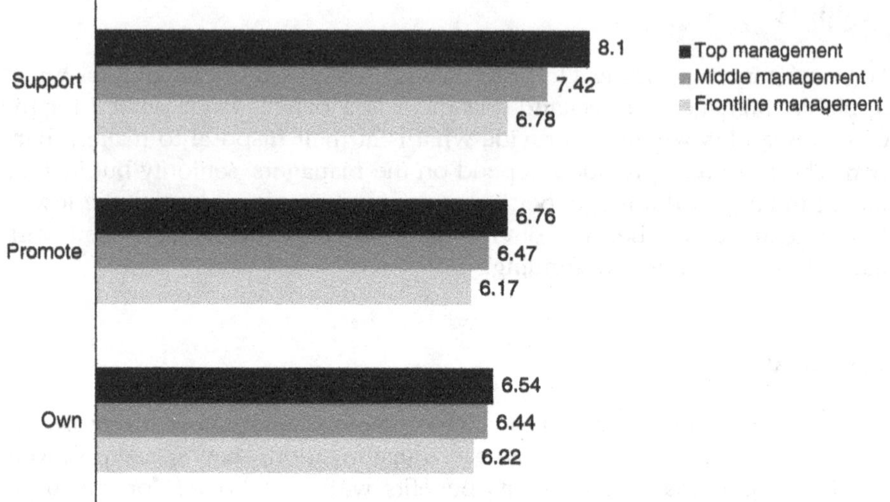

FIGURE 7.1 Management activities to support, promote, and own the change.

Why Are Top Management So Highly Engaged?

Previous research, studies, and models agree that management is crucial for role-modeling behavioral and culture changes.[6] However, most of these models focus on the role of top management and indicate that engagement needs to happen at the highest level.

Focusing on top-level management over the other levels is a common consequence of the traditional focus on top-down waterfall transformation approaches. Indeed, top management involvement is vital at the earlier stages of a transformation. The processes described in Chapters 4 and 5 – setting goals, defining the approach, and securing or providing the funding and resources for the transformation – are often completed by C-level management.

A very natural consequence is that the team spends a lot of time meeting, talking, and engaging with the organization's top management. If you are currently working on a transformation, count last month's hours and how much time you spent preparing and meeting with top managers compared to meeting with middle and frontline managers.

In our interviews, we encountered examples of projects that have skillfully used top management. Several projects found it indispensable to get top management to repeatedly restate the reason for the change; handle communication with external stakeholders; host and attend webinars, conferences, and town halls; give interviews to the media; keep the board updated; and remove procurement roadblocks.

Case Study: CEO Getting Stuck in a Transformation

In a recent project, one of our team approached the chief executive officer of a global bank. The bank was running a project to replace nearly all its outdated core banking systems. Core banking systems are the ones that run the products – current accounts, saving accounts, credit cards, investment products, managing customer identities, and so on. Every bank runs a large and complex suite of different systems.

Having done our research, one of us talked with the CEO, and we informed him that the amount of organizational change meant that he needed to own the project. To our surprise, the busy CEO replied: "I understand that. I can give you half a day a week. But I used to be the chief financial officer. I am not an IT specialist, and I am not a change specialist. You need to tell me what to do. So, what do you want me to do?"

As we were surprised by this answer, we told the CEO that we would devise a plan and get back to him.

The next day, we had a group research meeting. Having been put on the back foot by the conversation with the CEO, we used the time to brainstorm what we would ask him to do.

Our ideas included:

- Attend the steering committee meetings and read the briefing notes – do not send your deputy.
- Hold a town hall meeting with frontline staff.
- Help us with politics – we need to get some reluctant middle managers to buy into the project.
- Make sure funding for the project is protected from budget cuts.
- Read the status reports and briefing notes.

One day the CEO made time to help test cases looking at data migration; the impact was brilliant. The project team got a massive morale and motivational boost seeing their CEO showing interest and getting involved (even though they later reran the tests the CEO did because they did not entirely trust that they had been done correctly).

One project leader commented that the most powerful message the CEO communicated to the rest of the organization was that they were also users of the system – they experienced their own frustrations with it and had expectations for a better version.

Our findings lead to a crucial question in your transformation: What would you want your CEO to do if they offered you a half day of their time every week? What would you want middle managers and frontline managers to do?

We agree that top managers need to engage with projects; they have an essential role to play. However, our data show that the most crucial group is frontline managers.

Our research – as measured on a scale of 1 to 10 through our interviews and surveys – shows that the higher up the management chain you go, the more likely it is that management will engage with the project. However, despite being the least engaged on average, it is the frontline managers whose engagement has the greatest impact on the transformation's success.

In fact, our data show that only the level of frontline engagement has a statistically significant impact on transformation success. However, the data also show significant covariation among all three levels of management. In our findings, the more top and middle managers were engaged in the transformation, the more the frontline managers were engaged as well (Figure 7.2).

The engagement of frontline managers is crucial because the success of a transformation is dependent on successfully encouraging end users to accept

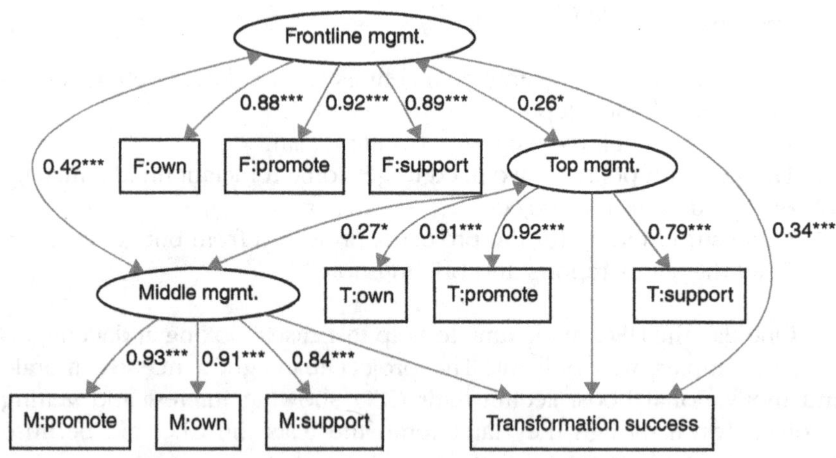

FIGURE 7.2 Effects of management ownership and transformation success (T = top management, M = middle management, F = frontline management). The figure shows only coefficients of statistically significant paths. Stars indicate statistical significance: *** $p \leq 0.001$, ** $p \leq 0.01$, * $p \leq 0.05$.

and use the new systems and processes. As discussed in Chapters 4 and 5, frontline managers are the closest and best equipped to support end users by embracing the change and handling their concerns after the technology has gone live.

Once project and change managers have completed their roles and moved on, frontline managers will take up the role of realizing the benefits of the transformation. They will do this by supporting end users to buy into the changes and helping them with doubts or concerns. (Chapter 9 examines this topic in more detail.) Frontline manager ownership makes it statistically significantly more likely that the organization will achieve the transformation's intended benefits.

Securing these benefits can happen only if frontline managers take ownership of their role in the project. For this to happen, frontline management needs to have bought into the project's benefits themselves; how can they inspire someone else to believe in something that they don't believe in themselves?

Therefore, we need to be clear about "What is in it for me, the frontline manager?" These managers must also feel equipped, empowered, and informed to own their part in the transformation.

As in our encounter with the banking CEO seeking our advice on best supporting the transformation in the earlier story, the first step is to be clear about what we want from the frontline managers. What do we want them to do? What do we want them to say? What do they need to hear? How do they need to feel?[7]

Then we can start devising our engagement. In the following chapters, we cover three essential aspects of their involvement in the transformation. We need their help communicating, training, and establishing trust with end users. What support do we provide to frontline management in these areas and beyond?

Engaging Directly with Frontline Managers Isn't Always Straightforward

So, if the frontline managers can have the most impact on a transformation's long-term success, why are they underutilized, if not neglected? From the perspective of transformation and project leaders, interacting with frontline managers directly is comparatively hard, simply because there are great many of them, and they are busy running their teams.

A large international organization undertaking an ambitious digital transformation will have many teams – each with its own trusted and familiar frontline manager – spread out over a wide area. Top management, however, will be a much smaller circle of people, typically all concentrated in the head office.

It is far easier for the project leader to approach a C-level executive and provide them with a well-prepared presentation on the project's progress, which the executive can present at a town hall meeting, than to engage with the entire frontline management team. This team might consist of hundreds of frontline managers, who will all have their own opinions and concerns about the transformation.

An approach we successfully applied with one global organization that allowed us to keep frontline management engaged promptly was sending any significant communication to frontline managers several days before it was sent to the entire organization. We also provided a list of anticipated questions and potential answers for the frontline managers. In this way, we could keep frontline management informed and make managers feel confident that they will not be surprised by important events and announcements.

It also gave these managers an opportunity to pass any concerns up the chain to their superiors in middle management, if needed, which would give them more trust and a sense of security in the transformation.

Nowadays, any large-scale construction project has a 24/7 telephone helpline and email inbox for questions and complaints from the general public. Why do we not see that in digital transformations?

What the Data Say

In our interviews, we collected a list of activities that top, middle, and frontline managers were involved in for each transformation. Communication was the most frequent activity for every level of management. For this reason, a critical activity is equipping managers with the tools and messages to communicate, tailored to their level.

The second most frequent role of management is setting strategic direction and making strategic decisions. In our interviews, these roles were predominantly the purview of top and middle managers; frontline managers were less involved in the decision-making process.

The third most frequent activity was securing funding and resources, again an activity that is important across levels of authority. Yet the actual engagement takes a different form: Frontline managers helped projects get access to very specific persons, while middle and top management operated on a more abstract level of setting budgets.

Finally, some very specific activities differed by the level of authority. Benefits realization was a key concern for middle and frontline managers. In the transformations we studied, frontline managers were heavily involved in designing, testing, co-creating and conducting training, providing postimplementation support, and acting as pilot users. In several transformations, they were active challengers of developed solutions and processes.

Top management was useful in some activities, such as handling the media and external stakeholders; hosting events, town halls, and webinars; and listening to the organization.

Asking the Right Questions

Another reason frontline managers are not used to their best advantage is that different management levels require different management styles. For this reason, it is difficult for top-level managers to communicate effectively with their frontline managers about the change.

Top management is skilled at running the business; they are trusted with running entire departments, divisions, or the company itself because they are good at it. However, when it comes to managing change and supporting people with these changes, they might lack the hands-on, up-to-date experience required to work effectively.

Problems arise when top management thinks that they are supposed to have the answer to everything. This need to have all the answers all the time means that they might not be asking the right questions to middle management, questions that, in turn, get asked to frontline management.

Case Study: Reducing Processing Time for Complaints

[Tom] An example of the value of top management asking questions and not holding themselves accountable for having all the answers was an incident in a management meeting for a company I was consulting with. A new IT solution was being introduced, and one of the processes required cutting down the time to handle and respond to complaints.

The goal was for responses to complaints to be delivered within 24 hours. Designing an IT solution for this seemed easy enough; the technical processes seemed straightforward too. However, handling the complaints required two separate departments to interact with each other. The service levels *between* the departments had to be considered.

(continued)

(continued)

It turned out that management had never actually considered this interaction between departments before; the need for this dialogue was not realized until we were simulating the new business processes. The managers in the meeting could not agree on how that interaction would work; they did not have the data required to agree on what was needed for Department A to successfully hand over the complaint to Department B in time.

Eventually, it was discovered that for delivery to happen in 24 hours, Department A needed to pass the complaint onto Department B in under eight hours. The managers also realized that they needed to start asking questions about interactions between departments in order to optimize the company's workflow in general.

The key to success here was encouraging joint ownership between Departments A and B. Ensuring that both departments held equal responsibility for cross-departmental interactions helped ensure the interaction was completed successfully.

This shared responsibility was, in fact, far more effective than the alternative: creating a specific managerial role governing the flow of information between departments. Instead of encouraging managers from the two existing departments to engage and cooperate, all this achieves is creating a third department to be interacted with. In our experience, operating within the existing structures is far more effective than adding an additional layer.[8]

There is nothing wrong with admitting that you do not have all the information to hand. When transformations are open about the things they do not know, frontline managers learn that they have valuable information to contribute, and they will start developing a sense of emotional investment and ownership toward the transformation.

Moreover, top management can help the project run more efficiently by being more willing to ask the people beneath them the right questions. In the case study we just examined, if the need to optimize interdepartmental interactions had not been discovered until late in development or after going live, the transformation's successful implementation might have been compromised, or at least delayed.

If top management is willing to ask questions of middle management and frontline management, it directs top managers' focus in the correct direction. When the focus is correct, the necessary feedback from user involvement described in Chapter 6 will be collected and acted on.

Case Study: Time Management and Delegation

Another thing that interferes with management's ability to engage with a project is balancing this engagement with their other duties. Kim recently interacted with a chief financial officer suffering from this problem – she was struggling to balance her ownership of projects with her C-level duties.

The CFO was remarkably invested in this specific project – she was the sponsor and wanted to be highly engaged with it. However, she was also the sponsor for 14 other projects simultaneously. Ultimately, she had to admit that she couldn't continue to actively own 15 projects at the same time and also carry out her management responsibilities. Eventually, she had to consider delegating ownership of her projects.

While change is interesting and exciting, it is crucial to recognize that it is impossible to do everything. As a leader, your priority should be to own your commitments. If there is no capacity or bandwidth available to execute a project, then part of leadership involves saying no.

Killing a project that could become an incredible innovation is hard – sometimes saying no is the hardest part of leadership, in fact. However, if the time and resources are not available, taking on more projects only leads to overload, reducing the efficiency and effectiveness of active projects across the board.

A Drastic Approach to Avoid Overload

The issue at the heart of the previous case study is all too common. In public sector projects in the United Kingdom, each project has two distinct roles: the project sponsor – called the senior responsible owner (SRO) – and the project director (PD).

The role of the SRO is outward-facing: dealing with stakeholders internal and external to the government and the media, setting direction, and shaping the project. The role of the PD is delivery-focused. A common practice evolved where one SRO managed several projects – in some cases, four or six such projects – all worth hundreds of millions of pounds.

Sponsoring several projects while running parts of the organization was overstretching the SROs. The unit in the Infrastructure and Projects Authority that oversees and guides all major projects made an important change.

The unit mandated that SROs commit 80% of their time to projects, at least during the planning and design stage, when critical decisions are made. No one knows whether 80% is the correct number, but the new guidance sent a strong signal to all departments that the SRO role is not just as a figurehead.

> ## Case Study: Communicating with Frontline Managers
>
> [Astrid] If the C-level managers are unable or unwilling to take ownership of a task, it can prevent essential steps in the project from happening. An example was consulting a company whose top management could not take ownership of crucial communication regarding a significant project.
>
> All the C-level managers agreed that the project was important and wanted influence and ownership over it. However, as we discuss in Chapter 8, communication is vital in a project. For this project, a 10-slide presentation to the frontline managers in the organization was needed. While top management agreed that this presentation was important, nobody could or was willing to create and present it.
>
> This was a struggle. Someone needed to give this presentation. Without it, frontline management would have been unaware of the project and the change.
>
> Middle management could cover this responsibility. Communicating with the entire frontline management team is a difficult task, so top management equipping middle management to pass the information along might be a far more effective use of the resources of top management and middle management.

Being aware of when to delegate responsibilities is also part of taking ownership. As we have been discussing, different levels of management contribute differently to a transformation. Top-level management must recognize when someone else can offer more value and delegate responsibilities.

Otherwise, top-level managers risk micromanaging the project or, worse, slowing the project down dramatically because decisions never get made. If a project is being micromanaged by top-level management, no space is being created for other managers to take ownership of the roles and responsibilities for which they are potentially better equipped.

Micromanagement by top-level managers also does not demonstrate trust in the transformation team's ability to support lower-level managers, which prevents middle and frontline managers from developing a positive emotional attachment to the project. Lack of such attachment can then cause a ripple effect of disengagement and totally threaten the success of the transformation.

Prioritization of Ownership

Balancing the various responsibilities and tasks that managers have on their plates can be difficult. Sometimes managers don't have time to own a transformation or because they have other, more pressing issues to worry about.

Ensuring these responsibilities are balanced correctly makes it easier for management to own the things that need owning. If given a choice between a task with an abstract long-term benefit and a fire in front of you that needs putting out, you will prioritize the fire every time.

To encourage ownership, be selective about your asks and provide focus. Engaging leaders of the organization and ensuring that they own the transformation is a collaborative process. Yet we heard in our interviews that establishing ground rules and sometimes being very literal about what you need for the transformation is a worthwhile investment.

Case Study: A Social Contract

[Alex] One project manager we interviewed had a creative solution: Draw up a two-page manual for senior, middle, and frontline managers. The manual spelled out what the project required from each manager, what they were expected to do, and how much time it would require. It also spelled out what they got in return – the project's intended benefits.

The manual evolved over the years, learning from every project and adding lessons.

Another project manager described a similar, slightly less formal approach: "Whenever I work with a new C-suite executive, I tell them that I will run the project for them under one condition: Help me when I ask for help, do not help me when I don't ask."

Case Study: Prioritizing Safety in a North Sea Offshore Drilling Company

[Tom] We worked on a culture transformation in a North Sea offshore drilling company. The aim was to strengthen the safety culture of the organization. The transformation needed to balance profit and productivity with security and safety.

At this company, safety and security were very important to the organization – they were part of their values. For this reason, top management wanted to ensure that every level of the organization owned its responsibilities regarding safety. They did this by making safety a regular focus in communications and meetings.

(continued)

In any organization, if the transformation is truly important and offers long-term benefits, it is important to make it clear that it is a priority – it will require active focus and attention. Such focus and attention might involve deprioritizing other tasks and responsibilities to make it easier for frontline and middle managers to own their parts in ensuring its success.

We all know of companies that, during the early phases of COVID-19, had to improvise, work creatively, and cut corners to continue to operate. Transforming to tap into the collective organizational desire to be successful will undoubtedly be harder without crisis-focusing minds, but wouldn't it be great to achieve the same drive?

Our data show that middle and frontline managers are key to benefit realization. Frontline managers will be the first to hear about problems with new systems and processes. They need to take ownership and be able to deal with the problems instead of delegating them upward, as was the pattern observed by Smith in the 1930s textile mills discussed in Chapter 1. We discovered that the key role of middle management is to hold their organization to account.

In one transformation we studied, the team created a list of "the good and the bad" managers. Champions who implemented the change were celebrated, and the company identified laggards who needed to be held accountable. While the naming-and-shaming approach is certainly a last resort, it was effective in encouraging accountability in this transformation.

Case Study: Metropolitan Police Force

[Alex] The Metropolitan Police is a particularly time-poor organization. Frontline managers often interact directly with their entire team for just the 10-minute duration of the operational briefing at the start of each shift. After that time, everyone disperses to walk their beat or get on with their work.

A deeply shocking incident in 2005 – an officer shot and killed an innocent man[9] – required the organization to make immediate culture change a top priority. The action taken and how the culture transformation was presented made clear the seriousness with which the incident was being taken by management.

The Met did this by spending two days across the organization focusing on the situation and the changes required. Everyone was given two days to sit down and discuss the judicial findings from the investigation of the incident: what the findings meant for the Met, what could be done to prevent a similar event in the future, and what people would like to do differently.

This intervention was a complete right turn from how things were usually run. The fact that such a time-poor organization allotted two full days to focus on culture change over everything else drove home the seriousness of the situation. Taking such a drastic step made it clear that everyone, at all levels, was taking ownership of ensuring things that changed – not just sweeping it under the rug and continuing as normal. While it was a strong signal at the time and had the desired effect, some 20 years after the event, the Met is still struggling with culture change.

What Will Transferring Ownership Look Like in a Transformation?

Ultimately, frontline and middle managers will own the responsibilities they feel equipped to own and manage, responsibilities that are a priority for their work. This fact ties in to several other levers that we discuss in other chapters of this book.

The first step in transferring ownership of organizational change is to establish a culture in which active engagement is encouraged. It is easy for managers to pass a responsibility down the line and then trust that it is being followed through on. By actively asking questions and showing interest in progress, top management directly focuses down the management chain and receives feedback back up the chain.

This active interest encourages frontline managers to take responsibility for ensuring they have the information they need to interact with their teams.

There is a catch, however. In some of our interviews, we heard that engaging with frontline managers created noise and distractions. Be prepared for this and have strategies to help this communication stay effective. In Chapter 8, we discuss ways to handle tricky communication situations.

The second step is equipping frontline managers with the necessary tools and information. According to our data, transformations are more successful when frontline managers support and inform end users about the new systems and changes. If frontline managers are actively trained and supported on the changes and new processes of the specific transformation, they can pass that experience and support farther down the chain.

The third step is to consider management in communications. Frontline management will be the main point of contact between end users and the organization. As a result, they will be the ones who need to clarify the message and address any doubts or concerns. One effective way to help managers buy in to a project is by giving them a first look at any communication being sent out.

This first look gives them a warning of any significant changes or events, which allows them to begin preparing and processing any information or requirements they might have. Part of good communications involves creating a forum or other such space for managers to discuss the changes and the transformation with each other. Creating a peer network allows them to share any concerns or questions they may have themselves and help each other with the transformation.

Considering frontline managers' needs allows communication to occur in a more controlled or effective way, a topic we examine further in Chapter 8. This approach also allows management to interact and engage with each other. Seeing that they have the space and authority to resolve any doubts or concerns and to influence the transformation encourages an increased sense of project ownership.

CHAPTER 8

Lever #5: Effective Communication

In this modern world, people are often bombarded by information from all angles. Because there is so much going on in an active organization, there is a constant battle for employees' attention. Often an overwhelming amount of noise stops effective communication.

Have you ever been required to sit quietly through unending meetings listening to presentations in which no dialogue is happening? Or have you opened your inbox and been greeted by a mountain of unread newsletters, updates, or surveys? Often organizations' communication channels are overloaded with information.

Because the critical messages end up mixing in with the dull, generic broadcasts, most messages end up in the mental spam folder, as employees are almost conditioned to feel no urgency to read large corporate broadcasts.

A survey found that Intel employees receive, on average, 350 emails per week and executives at Intel up to 300 a day! Respondents judged that nearly one-third of the messages they received were unnecessary. The high volume of emails comes at a high cost – in the same study, Microsoft found that it takes company employees, on average, 24 minutes to return to their task after being interrupted by an email.[1]

Another reason behind ineffective communications is that the communicator does not necessarily consider the value and cost to the receiver. From a project perspective, a message saying "56% of the User Acceptance Testing test cases have been passed! Yay!" might be exciting and interesting to us; however, in the world of the end users – who most likely have no context on the technical aspects of the transformation – who cares about that?

The same goes for all the initiatives taking place in the organization. Anything from reorganization to a new sales initiative or an HR leadership model might be transmitted throughout the organization; however, it might not be relevant to the people receiving it, so it only adds to the already loud background noise.

The sheer volume of information being broadcast to people is overwhelming and makes effective communication and dialogue difficult – and when you are trying to roll out successful change in a large organization, the information overload can be deadly.

In an organization where each employee gets 200 emails in one day, employees will not be able to interact with each other. An urgent email that requires the recipient to respond might not be able to cut through all that noise and open up the right kind of dialogue to ensure people are clear on what is changing, why it is changing, and how it is going to change.

Case Study: Overwhelmed by Constant Broadcasting

[Kim] I experienced this issue in action when I was in a Danish organization with one of the largest marketing budgets in Denmark. We were trying to figure out the best way to get a message out to the whole organization. One suggestion was to produce a flyer to put on each person's desk. However, when we ran this idea past some of the people we were trying to communicate with, we realized that it wouldn't work.

They told us that they were tired of things appearing on their desks. They felt like something – a croissant or dice with logos printed – appeared on their desks weekly. This constant stream of small gifts attached to flyers and leaflets about new IT systems was noisy and overwhelming to them.

While the gifts might have been intended to make communication "fun," the actions ultimately failed.

This approach was overwhelming because multiple projects, initiatives, and transformations were competing for end users' attention, using escalating methods to outdo each other. It is nearly inevitable that multiple transformations will happen simultaneously, but in such cases, a coordinated approach to communication might be more effective than each project communicating separately.

In this case, we first tried to focus the team's effort on coordinating communications with the other transformations. Then, based on our research, we realized that we should stop communicating and start talking. So, we shifted our approach fully to enable frontline managers to communicate better and engage in open dialogue about the change.

Most of us know what makes communication effective. We decided to investigate the three most challenging factors in our research: Communication needs to be targeted, dialogue-based, and focus on positive reinforcement.

1. *Targeted* – Not everyone needs to know the same information, and not everyone processes information in the same way. Some people prefer tables of data, others want visualizations, and still others prefer to read. An organization-wide broadcast that is addressed to everyone fails to address the needs of the individual and often gets ignored.

   There is little point in being asked to process information that has nothing to do with you. Most people involved in a transformation are busy and have certain priorities. They must be given a good reason to invest time in engaging with communications and prioritize one communication over other important things.

   Knowing your audience, identifying who needs to get the message, and addressing them expressly and in their language is far more effective than sending the same blast emails to all staff.[2] By using targeted communication, you are more likely to capture your target audience's attention and engagement, which means you are more likely to successfully open a channel of communication that provides you with what you need.

2. *Dialogue-based* – The easiest way to know that you have successfully targeted and engaged someone is if you are getting answers back. One of the main benefits of having an open discussion and dialogue around a project implementation is the ability to receive feedback. This finding was made by Smith[3] in the 1930s (see Chapter 1), and it still holds today.

   Dialogue helps build a trusting relationship – End users or stakeholders feel that their doubts, concerns, and input are being recognized, appreciated, and addressed. It also means you are gathering the information you need to optimize the implementation.

3. *Positive reinforcement* – In the 1930s, B.F. Skinner discovered that positive reinforcement created behavioral change more effectively than punishment.[4] This insight has long been adopted in change communication, where messages focus on positive reinforcements such as celebrating champions and early success stories.

   Positive reinforcement is closely linked to managing benefits and presenting the achieved benefits of the change. In our data, we find that focusing on positive reinforcement helps with targeting communications. By personalizing the focus of the message to something recipients find relevant, they will be more likely to prioritize engaging with the message (Figure 8.1).

Our data also show that focusing on positive reinforcement leads to more dialogue and better targeting of communications, likely because finding and sharing stories that reinforce new behaviors increases the level of listening more than mere telling about change in the abstract does.

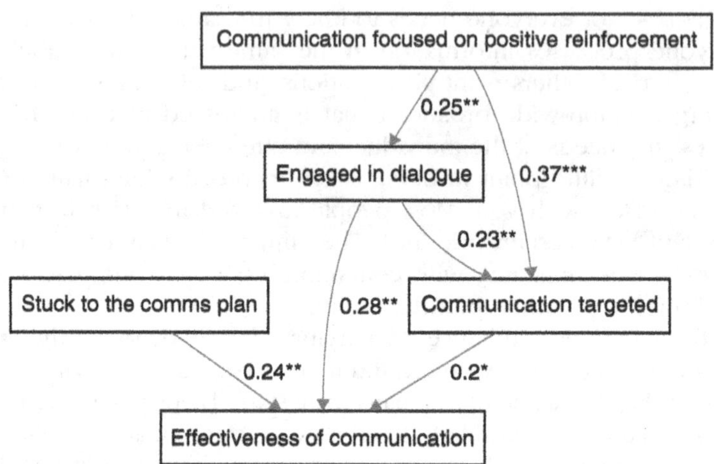

FIGURE 8.1 Model of communication effectiveness. The figure shows only coefficients of statistically significant paths. Stars indicate statistical significance: *** $p \leq 0.001$, ** $p \leq 0.01$, * $p \leq 0.05$.

Does This Mean We Need a Communication Plan?

When considering the impact of having a defined communication plan or strategy, the data are not particularly clear on the benefits of having or not having such a plan; 83% of organizations we studied did have one, so we do not have much conclusive data on its absence.

In our interviews, we found that most communication plans were relatively basic. Most plans simply defined the frequency or points in time that would trigger communication – for example, four weeks before going live. Some plans were based on stakeholder analysis.

Only one transformation we analyzed had quarterly review meetings to calibrate and fine-tune communication using measurable results the company intended its communications to achieve.

What was absolutely clear, though, was that simply having a communication plan to refer to was not enough. In the same way that having a change management strategy is not enough, people must actively and consistently put the communication plan into action.

Our data show that nearly all transformations, 83%, had a communication plan. Of these projects with communication plans:

- 77% stuck to their plans to a great degree.
- 12% executed the plan exactly as it was without changes.

Who Needs to Be the Person Communicating?

Determining who should be in charge of communicating with individuals – stakeholders and end users – is complicated.

We asked who the end users of a project see as the primary communicators of organizational change. The project manager was most frequently mentioned, followed by top management and the change team (Figure 8.2).

In some transformations we studied, communication was well balanced among various communicators. Depending on the transformation, sometimes the key communicator was the product or process owner. In one highly entertaining example, the team created an artificial persona for the new system and made this persona the key communicator of changes.

Our data show that the communication professional – whether an external freelancer representing the temporary project team or an internal employee from the permanent organization's communications department – was generally the most effective communicator, measured on the average effectiveness of the communication.

However, as we discussed in Chapter 7, communication is the key to engaging management from the top of the organization down to the frontline managers. The same holds true, of course, for securing the buy-in of end users. As we discuss in detail in Chapter 10, a key requirement of transformations is to create and maintain trust-based relationships.

When we chart the data by the average effectiveness of the communication efforts on the horizontal axis and the level of trust built with end users and stakeholders, both values were measured from 1 (the least) to 10 (the

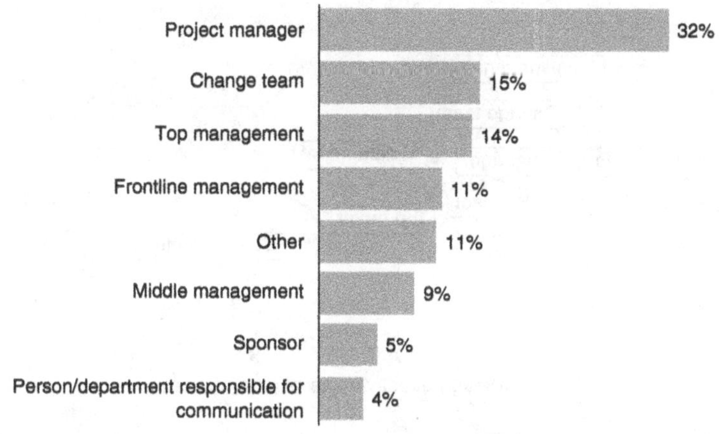

FIGURE 8.2 Who did end users perceive as the primary communicator?

most) (Figure 8.3).The effectiveness of the communication was rated by how well the project leader felt the recipient understood the message that had been given.

The graph shows a problem. When communication professionals are the key communicators of the change, communication effectiveness is highest; however, the trust the project built with end users and stakeholders is lowest on average.

Conversely, when frontline managers were the key communicators of the change, the effectiveness of the communications was lowest, yet these transformations had the highest average level of trust-based relationships.

However, as we discussed in Chapter 7, frontline managers are an unquestionably valuable resource when interacting with end users. In part, this is because end users' managers often are far more able to tailor the message to users' needs, making the communication targeted.

The preexisting relationship between the manager and the individual also allows a dialogue to happen far more easily than if it were coming from someone new with whom end users do not have a personal relationship.

A colleague who is in the military and has served in Afghanistan several times puts it quite well. When you ask him who he listens to and who he takes his orders from, he will tell you, "I don't listen to the general; I listen to my platoon lead!"

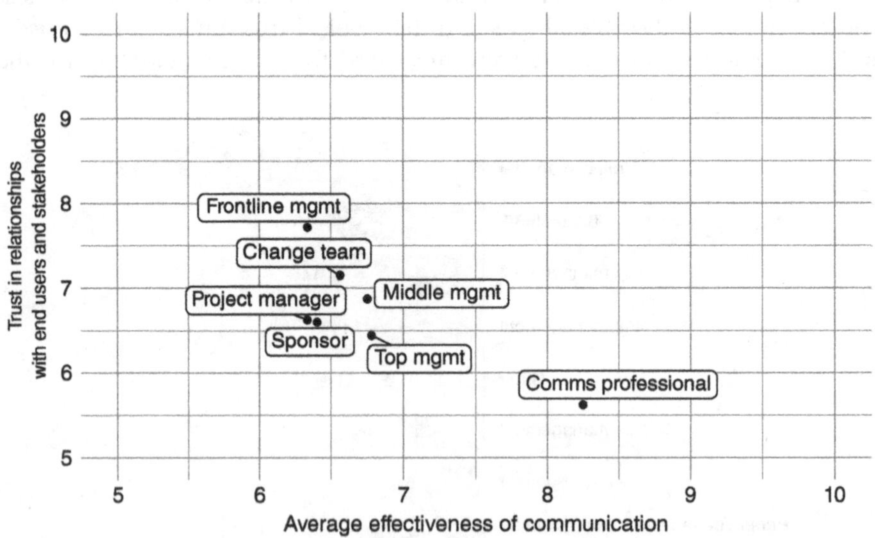

FIGURE 8.3 Effectiveness of communication and the relation to the established levels of trust by different primary communicators of the change.

Thus, the critical finding from our research on who should be the primary communicator is clear: frontline managers. The project team's responsibility is not to rely on the communications experts; instead, the team should use the experts to prepare, support, and coach to enable the already trusted voices in the organization.

In our interviews, we found transformations created highly effective communication by establishing clear roles and responsibilities and clearly defined concrete activities. These projects then prepared frontline managers with training and coaching as well as providing materials, lists of key messages, and the like.

Targeting Communication and Making It Relevant

Understanding your audience and targeting it effectively with tailored messaging can make a huge difference to the success of transformations. What one end user wants to know about often differs from what interests an end user from a different team or the person leading the transformation. What they need to know is how a message is relevant to them.

A helpful framework to make communication relevant is to understand the barriers to change. Our Oxford colleague Steve New suggests approaching the analysis like a movie detective.[5] Do users lack the means, the opportunity, or the motive for the intended behavioral change to happen?

If the gap is predominantly *means-based,* then the solution centers on capabilities through training, system capabilities, or capabilities built into processes. Therefore, communication needs to focus on these new capabilities and how they might be acquired.

Suppose the gap falls into the *opportunity* category (i.e., users have the know-how and are motivated to change but lack opportunities). In that case, communication needs to talk about prompt behaviors and habits or share examples of how others have made time and created the space for changes. One of the cases we studied – a bank – celebrates examples of users who carved out opportunities for themselves. One of our interviewees referred to the famous NASA Pirates[6] and Lockheed's Skunkworks[7] when we talked about their transformation. In these classic examples of change, a team formed to do things differently. The NASA Pirates developed new software for mission control. Lockheed's Skunkworks developed new aircraft designs, starting with the P-38 Lighting in 1939. Because the Pirates and the Skunkworks wanted to do things differently, they set up a special-purpose organization outside the existing organization with a different set of values, a different culture, and new ways of collaborating.

Our interviewee brought up the Pirates and Skunkworks as an illustration of how bold moves by employees can create opportunities for change. Subsequently, the communications of the transformation focused on stories of the bank's pirates – individuals who actively worked with and around the existing structures to create opportunities to bring about change.

If the barrier to change is *motivation*, then communication must target incentivization (the "What's in it for me?"), persuasion, education, and even coercion.

In our interviews, one project leader shared that they executed the project plan, but "it left [me with] the feeling that something or someone was missing sometimes. I was often told 'We don't understand what he's saying.'" This was the moment the project rethought its approach to communication and started to analyze its audience in earnest.

In our research, we found that transformations frequently struggled with communication targeting. Most knew that targeting was a good idea but ended up communicating one-size-fits-all messages. The transformations that took a more granular approach targeted their communication at the team level or tailored one-to-one communications through the frontline managers.

The one-to-one communication approach through frontline managers is a critical – if not a legal – requirement when job losses are part of the change.

Is It All About Positive Messages?

When we looked through the research for organizational change, we repeatedly found that communications need to focus on positive reinforcement.[8] What that means in practical terms was best explained by one of our interviewees:

> "We did have the data to take a punitive approach – we could make examples of bad users, but we avoided that. We used positive examples and tried to encourage instead of threatening users. That was a conscious decision."

Other transformations focused their positive message on improvements in user experience as a very tangible positive outcome of the change. Some projects tried to celebrate early wins – for example, the first sales order process through the new system and process.

However, in our interviews, we found that most transformations stuck to the facts. They took a timider approach and communicated factual messages rather than positive reinforcement messages.

In all cases, we heard that honest and open communication is vital. One interviewee explained vividly: "Unfortunately, the project's premise was that we had an inferior product. But on the other hand, we focused on a better-integrated system in the organization."

The most thought-provoking transformations we studied started with lots of positive messages. Yet, as with many technology projects, once the project hit roadblocks and started to slip, keeping up the positive spirit became increasingly difficult. For us, the key insight from these interviews is that when planning communication, we need to consider what to communicate if the project starts to fall behind or gets negative feedback. Being caught unawares makes a bad situation worse.

A few inspiring transformations preempted this particular communication challenge by focusing all communications around the "fail fast" theme. When the project encountered difficulties – in this case, the first product iterations had a much lower uptake in the market than expected – what might have been a failure became a moment to double down on efforts.

Case Study: Political Campaign – Targeting the Message

[Alex] Some of the public sector projects we have encountered in our research have cleverly adapted classic tools from political campaigns and marketing to help optimize their communications.[9] One example is adapting A/B testing to internal communications.

The first Obama election campaign changed how political campaigning worked quite drastically. The campaign leaders worked out that they could measure the effectiveness of campaign emails by including an easily achievable call to action – often making a very small donation between $1 and $5.

They tested whether certain emails were more likely to elicit the reactions and interactions they wanted: emails from Michelle Obama talking about healthcare or emails from Barack Obama himself setting out his agenda for job creation. They wanted to know which was more likely to increase engagement and result in a donation.

Public sector organizations implementing this strategy realized that the same logic behind writing political campaign emails to raise funds applied to their change communication. Instead of unthinkingly sending out information, they defined a desired and measurable outcome from the communication. If that outcome didn't happen, they knew they needed to optimize their message.

(continued)

(continued)

Doing this involved asking themselves some questions:

- What success stories do users read?
- Do we want users to book a training slot? If so, what header, message, and sender works best?

In the case of this public sector project, the concern was about stakeholder engagement rather than end user engagement. The desired outcome was that stakeholders demonstrate support for the project – by signing a letter of support, representing the project at a town hall meeting, or similar actions. To achieve this outcome, the transformation's leaders needed to discover the narrative and approach that would inspire stakeholders to buy into the project.

If the communications did not achieve the intended outcome, the team went back to the drawing board and analyzed what could be revisited – how could they better target the stakeholders who had not responded? Over time, and thanks to having a specifically measurable metric for successful communication, they were able to improve the message and make it more effective. The key to this improvement was identifying and targeting a behavioral response. If that didn't exist, they created one.

Often communication aims to have someone act on the information they have been given. Suppose you can shape the message and call to action to achieve this better while making the desired result measurable. In such cases, the communications you send become more effective and pointless information that adds to the noise is reduced.

Enabling Dialogue

Remember the critical insight from Smith's 1930s study of technology change in the textile mills (see Chapter 1)? Whenever dialogue with end users was replaced by broadcast communication, the change ended in disaster.

The same point is still valid. As one of our interviewees put it, the mantra is "Make communication come to you!"

If you go into a conversation with the desire to provide full transparency and the person you are talking to doesn't care – perhaps they have no curiosity beyond whether it is a problem to them directly – you overwhelm them with too much information. Worse, if you assume they would not be interested, you might limit the chance for dialogue if they want more information.

What needs to be achieved is a dialogue that addresses their needs and provides them with the space and trust to ask questions. Giving them space to ask questions and interact with the solution – even if it is not fully implemented or complete yet – helps to build their confidence in the solution.

However, often it is difficult to engage in dialogue when your team has so much information to convey. One interviewee saw his team's interactions in meetings and decided that they had to change. This interviewee said: "I told them that from now on, in meetings, they can only do 20% of the talking and need to listen 80% of the time. We never got there. It was more like 50–50. Yet a big improvement to what was going on before."

In the transformations we studied, some created dialogue by having virtual sessions without agendas. These were just spaces for anyone to come and join and provide feedback or share questions and concerns.

Similarly, other teams conducted regular site visits – as one project leader put it, "We deliberately camped out in the different departments." Another one reflected: "We did a lot of travel to South Korea, where the implementation was struggling. It was great, and actually, we had the best conversations with users when we sat on the plane and traveled to the sites." Showing up in person to listen proved to be a very powerful approach.

Nearly half of the transformations in our study established a user forum or advisory council. Yet, the results were very mixed. For some projects, engaging with dialogue worked brilliantly. Others described their experience: "We had many changes in user representatives in our forums over time. So often we had to start back at the beginning – it felt like we lost a lot of time."

And one project faced another common concern: "There was opposition that we had to deal with. We dealt with that by listening to some of the employees who objected. It didn't seem reasonable to sit in a forum with them – it wasn't constructive."

The project leader further explained that suddenly, there was a lucky break: "We found this one employee who was good at communicating her frustrations. We made her the spokeswoman for the case handlers [the system's end users]. Shifting from a big forum to meetings with the spokeswoman was very constructive."

According to our interviews, the most effective way was to create focused dialogue and feedback. All transformations said that their most helpful dialogue occurred during testing and training.

Interacting with a prototype allows people to play with the new systems and provide valuable feedback – possibly identifying needs that the new system does not address yet or that the designers might not have been aware of. Even if the information is uncertain or confidential, providing what is currently available demonstrates and builds confidence and trust.

In our interviews, we repeatedly heard that sessions to test prototypes, demonstrate the new systems and processes, and even coworking sessions worked the best to gather feedback and listen to users.

Testing of prototypes, demonstrations, and coworking sessions worked particularly well because a straightforward process exists for adding any improvements or concerns raised in these sessions to the project's production pipeline. Nothing is worse than users raising concerns, having them noted, but the project rolls on without considering those concerns.

The second area where a lot of dialogue emerged was during training, particularly how-to training. We expand on training in Chapter 9. Yet one key concern that every transformation needs to consider early is how to collect feedback in training sessions and how that feeds into the project – feedback about the training and, more important, feedback about the change.

Some transformations we studied discovered the power of training too late. They got the most feedback and dialogue with users when they started training, but training occurred too late in the project for significant changes to be made.

Case Study: Genius Bars – Creating a Space for Dialogue

[Alex] A pharmaceutical company was consolidating its sales systems. Previously, its salespeople needed to use 14 IT systems, some of which could be accessed only in an office. The organization was trying to reduce that number to a single web app that worked in any location the salespeople traveled, a very reasonable motive for change with significant upsides for the organization.

To this organization, it was vital that the information needed to communicate to end users about this change was not lost to the noise of traditional broadcasting like emails, pamphlets, and the like. So the organization looked for alternative solutions.

It developed a solution inspired by the Apple Store's Genius Bars. Every salesperson knew the new sales system would be implemented in their region and office by a particular deadline. To help them prepare, a "Genius Bar" that offered daily training and personal support was put into every office.

For example, salespeople could sign up for a quick 20-minute training session on using the new system's functionality whenever it fit into their schedule. After the system went live, they could get support in seconds if they had any issues.

I shared this case study with the Metropolitan Police Force in London. Now the Met is implementing a similar system. To support the rollout of digitizing many of working practices, the Met opened "Tech Bars" in all its bigger offices. These Tech Bars can provide the precise level of information needed to teams when they need it without overwhelming them with too much noise.

In both organizations, the users loved the change.

Case Study: Microsoft Teams – Creating Relevance Through Curiosity

[Alex] One organization we looked at had a fascinating approach to stimulating communication. They did it by taking advantage of human nature and achieving their intended result by believing that people would naturally investigate things they are curious about.

The bank was rolling out a capability-building program in its IT department to shift to agile. It wanted to communicate the course's availability and convince people to enroll.

Leaders at the bank were ingeniously creative in how they did this, and it worked well enough that it did not add to the noise of constant information with regular emails reminding people to enroll. Instead, employees passing the course earned a badge displayed in their headshot on Microsoft Teams, the organization's internal messaging and virtual meeting software.

Gradually, people started to see these badges appear next to coworkers' names when they sent messages to each other or met in meetings. Naturally, people thought this was cool and interesting and became curious about how to earn the badge.

The great thing was that the first person they asked was a colleague who completed the course. What better ambassador could you possibly talk to? When they discovered the badge was for completing the course, they had a personal incentive to learn more and sign up.

5. When Communication Seems Tricky

There are two common challenges for change communication in organizations:

1. When we don't have all the information – often because things are uncertain at that stage in the transformation
2. When we are withholding information that we want to avoid communicating

As we discussed in Chapter 6, uncertainty is not a bad thing. Care is needed to prevent miscommunication, but trying to conceal uncertainty prevents you from making the most of the benefits of early engagement. Indeed, expressing the vulnerability that you don't have all the information yet – while making available what you do know already – is an opportunity to build trust and intimacy between the project and end users or stakeholders.

If you are not communicating anything, then you are not building the trust that we need for the transformation to be successful. An example we all experienced was during COVID-19. This was a period of immense uncertainty; nobody knew what was going to happen. Since this uncertainty was everywhere and everyone was in the same situation, everybody felt comfortable admitting they did not know what would happen.

No one was expected to have the answers. Changes were needed, and they were needed quickly. The willingness to be direct and honest about the lack of answers or information opened up communication – everyone was more willing to contribute what they could.

As one project leader put it (not for the purpose of this research):

> I had to enable thousands of call center workers to work from home. We had a little warning because everyone talked about lockdowns for a few months before they came into effect. My team knew the remote software worked badly, but we knew we could work on it later.
>
> However, my IT department turned overnight into this fulfillment warehouse to configure and ship out laptops. There were packages everywhere. The team, myself included, even loaded up our cars and drove them to employees.

The key was everyone understood the purpose and that a good-for-now solution is better than no solution.

The second trap occurs when something potentially unpleasant happens and management is unwilling to discuss it. If the change will result in layoffs or outsourcing, sending out the wrong message at the wrong time can cause a lot of trouble, not only with employees but also legally.

In our interviews, we heard one example of where this communication went wrong. Middle and frontline managers need to discuss layoffs with employees, yet they had not had those conversations.

Managers who avoid having potentially tricky discussions fail to treat team members with respect and dignity, which are needed for employees to trust employers. Employees will be aware that something is happening; in the absence of news, gossip and rumor will prevail. Gossip and rumor are not deviant acts of employees but are natural human response to pool information and intellectual ability to make sense of ambiguous and uncertain situations in order to take action.[10] Rumors spread if you don't fill the information gap or if the communicator is untrustworthy.

It is crucial to avoid the trap of reactive communication. Reactive communication happens when the transformation provides information only after gossip has emerged or questions have been raised. At the start of Chapter 6, we described an extreme example: the submarine-style transformation, which went dark until the very end. Reactive communication does communicate something though: that the transformation does not respect the end users' needs and damages the trust that enables effective communication to work. As the psychologist Paul Watzlawick once said: "One cannot not communicate."

A proactive approach is more productive, particularly for projects facing resistance or challenging questions. Putting the information and facts into the conversation up front and anticipating difficult questions by preparing answers beforehand prevents the conversation from getting out of hand. Otherwise, you will have to scramble to keep up, putting out fires as assumptions and rumors run wild.

Digital transformation ought to offer some benefit or efficiency gain; otherwise, there is no point in undertaking it. Even if the transformation is a regulatory compliance project known to increase the future cost of running the business, the cost of noncompliance is often seen as infinite. Subsequently, regulatory and compliance transformations often lack a focus on positive benefits.

However, as one project manager described:

> Whenever we received a regulatory requirement, I would turn the requirement into a positive business case – if the regulation is unclear and likely to change again, then let's do the absolute minimum using workarounds to invest less money than our competitors into compliance. On the other hand, if the regulation is clear and stable, let's overinvest to beat our competitors by having the cheapest run-the-business for this process.

Are You Listening?

We discovered a great way to think and frame communication and engagement in projects – inspired by talking to Irene Herremans, a professor at the University of Calgary, whose research focuses on how corporations and charities work with local communities and action groups. Herremans and her coauthors[11] developed a framework of engagement that spans a continuum from transactional, transitional, to transformational engagement.

We have adapted their idea of the engagement continuum to fit digital transformations (Table 8.1).

Transactional engagement is the most common form of engagement in the research of Bowen, Newenham-Kahindi, and Herremans. Transactional engagement is often called "public consultation," but it very rarely lives up to the name. Instead, it is one-sided communication in which communities are informed because the organization has to tick the box, such as when building a piece of infrastructure and planning notices pop up.

The classic example in the field of transformations is the textile mills we described in Chapter 1. The change was announced in a written statement on the notice board, and strikes and walkouts inevitably followed.

Transitional engagement, characterized by limited two-way communication, occurs most often with digital transformations. Stakeholders are engaged through focus groups and user representatives, and changes are communicated through a preplanned communication strategy.

A classic example of transitional engagement in transformation is the town hall. Get a large audience together, inform them about the changes, and answer the few questions that will come up. The large group will ensure that only limited interaction will take place. Ultimately, you can return to the stakeholders and unions and demonstrate that you held town halls in every location so that stakeholders will let the transformation progress to the next delivery stage. Only if the same question is asked repeatedly and you feel you do not have a good answer should you look into the issue.

TABLE 8.1 The different levels of stakeholder engagement in digital transformations.

	Transactional	Transitional	Transformational
Approach	"Investing"	"Building bridges"	"Changing the organization"
Idea	We make an investment that impacts the users; it will be better for them	We involve the user community	The user community is an integrative part of the project
Illustrative tactics	Information sessions, newsletters, posters	Dialogue, town halls, consultation meetings, feedback sessions	Joint project management, joint decision making, joint ownership
Communication balance	One way: project to community	Project-to-community greater than community-to-project communication	Equal balance of project-to-community and community-to-project communication
Nature of trust	Limited, if any	Evolving	Relational

Transformational engagement happens when a true partnership between local communities and corporations is established. As Irene explained to us, engagement is truly transformational only if changes happen on both sides – the organization changes, too, not just the local community.

Indeed, in our interviews, we heard about a common barrier to whole-hearted engagement with stakeholders: Engagement will lead to scope changes, delays, and unplanned extra costs to the project. Irene's research shows leaders who approach stakeholder engagement with these barriers in mind lose their social license to operate.

In one of the transformations we studied, the leaders actively sought ideas from the user group. First, the project worked with user representatives to solicit ideas and requirements. Once the scope of the change started to crystallize, the transformation engaged all users more broadly by holding an open house, where tables were set up with coffee and snacks and the transformation's leaders listened and answered users' questions.

The transformation leader added: "We had a very successful mailbox where people could come up with ideas and wishes for the project – there, we got over 200 inputs that were easy to group. For the best proposals, we held meetings with the proposers. Don't be afraid to make an open invitation."

Irene's research also showed that transformational engagement has no cost benefits – it is more expensive than transactional or transitional engagement. However, there are nonfinancial benefits: A clear link was found to longer-term improvements in evaluations of firms' reputation and corporate social responsibility.

Our data and interviews show some emerging practices of transformational engagement with the end user community.

A couple of transformations made users part of their steering committee – making end users an integrative part of setting strategic direction and making strategic choices.

Some projects were between transitional and transformational engagement, using coworking sessions and agile-style user representatives to support communication with their users.

Focus on Sharing the Cure, Not the Sugarcoating

by Lars Hancke

The perspective I bring toward communication is from my background in advertising – before I joined Implement nine years ago, I had almost 20 years of experience in advertising communication agencies. I am, in fact, the architect behind the positioning and marketing that Implement uses today.

(continued)

(continued)

Working at Implement was different from the communication roles I was used to. While we use some of the same tools you would otherwise use, we don't communicate externally. Instead of press-related or advertising-related communications, we focus on internal communication with stakeholders and end users.

As with external communication, our purpose is to tell a story. In advertising and marketing, you need to explain to the customer why they are investing in your product. People have realized that the same applies internally when communicating about a new project.

The "Big Why"

Creating storytelling in companies around a new project is a relatively new phenomenon. Simon Sinek's concept of the Golden Circle in his *Start with Why* has driven this realization and has been a revelation to the field of communication in the last decade.[12] Thanks to the Golden Circle, organizations have realized that you must prove the "why" for the change.

The "why" for the change has typically taken the form of the "big why" – the great purpose and big aspiration that everyone in the organization should rally behind and be proud of. This approach, however, has its failings.

One issue is that this approach loses sight of the practical details – the "what" and the "how" behind the project – creating uncertainty for those responsible for implementing the change. It is also a form of communication that is managed very "top down."

In cases that focus on the big why, top management has identified that a change needs to happen. Because the process itself might be an unpleasantly bitter pill for end users or stakeholders to swallow, top management provides a "big why" that sugar-coats the bad news.

As a result, top management does not explain what this pill contains or what it involves. In a worst-case scenario, an organizational Emperor's New Clothes arises: Top management believes it has a groundbreaking new approach solely because its "big why" has changed; end users, however, might see that the practical details are still 80% the same as the project from five years ago.

According to recent surveys, most top management believe they are overcommunicating. However, end users in the same companies typically say that top management is *under*communicating.[13] This discrepancy suggests that something is wrong with what is being said and how.

Communicating the "What" and the "How"

It helps when companies pay more attention to what is in the pill rather than sugarcoating it. Doing this involves moving away from focusing on the big why and bringing attention back to "what we will do" and "how we will do it."

What I find that end users need is not the great aspiration; it is the more minor details:

- What will happen?
- How can I be part of this transformation – where is my role?
- How can I make my voice count in the coming big change?

In my experience, what helps companies improve is the realization that what drives change is not the strategy but how people are involved in it.

Of course, this task is more complicated than just a company-wide broadcast. It involves clearly communicating to individuals what will happen and how *they* can participate. Often this enormous task is underestimated.

However, the Oxford research is unequivocal – change communication is an invaluable tool in creating and driving teams. Communication activities should be seen as externally advertising products in a competitive market.

How to "Advertise" the Change

Rather than a top-down approach of the big why, middle managers and frontline management need to be supported in change communication.

Top management receives a lot of support and focuses on communication. These managers receive training and have tools at their disposal. However, they typically delegate fixing problems to the leaders beneath them. This level of management does not receive support.

This position is often the worst one to be in – these leaders are under pressure from above and below. They also are not trained or supported in the disciplines underlying transformations from a change management and communication perspective.

Implement used to have a tagline that said "We are the missing link between management and employees." This gap between leadership and employees needs to be closed. Good communication, particularly from middle and frontline managers, helps reduce this gap's size.

If teams are nurtured and supported with different communication tools, you can build into them the ability to have someone who can address the little whys, hows, and whats from your end users.

What Makes Communication Effective?

Ultimately, the data offer overwhelming statistical evidence that communication cannot effectively support people through change processes if done as general broadcasts; transactional engagement does not work. All such engagement achieves is to encourage everybody to ignore the messages, since they have received so many without obvious relevance. There is no reason to engage with these unfocused message blasts.

Instead, we need to focus on dialogue that is more listening than telling. For actual change to happen, however, we need transformational engagement, which involves integrating our user and stakeholder communities in the transformation, making them jointly own the change. By making them part of decision making and project management, we effectively eliminate communication as it is typically thought about in our digital transformations.

CHAPTER 9

Lever #6: Effective Training

As established in Chapter 1, a transformation has two aspects. Both are important for ensuring the project's long-term success and should be prioritized equally.

1. *Technological change* focuses on the actual solution itself. It involves the work required to identify the best solution to the problem at hand and the requirements for implementation and operation. Successful management results in the solution itself being physically (so to speak) put in place.
2. *Organizational change* is about the people around the solution. This implementation style focuses on awareness of the solution and its benefits to individuals and the organization, in addition to training. Managing this aspect well allows end users and stakeholders to understand and adopt the solution, allowing long-term success.

As Chapter 1 explains, organizations often prioritize technology over organizational change. However, no transformation project will succeed in the long term without organizational change.

Effective training is an integral part of organizational change. Organizations know this; 90% of the digital transformations we investigated in our research had a training plan. However, the details of these plans varied greatly.

Training plans ranged from "We wrote down that the training will occur when and if needed. That was the extent of our plan" to training programs that had more than 100 individual courses and detailed plans so that more than 1,000 users would be trained within three days of going live.

While 90% of transformations in our data had a training plan, only 64% found their training effective, meaning that of the projects we surveyed, 24% had ineffective training plans and 10% did not have any plan.

Too often, we see organizations failing to get the most out of training and risking the success of their transformation as a result. One reason for this failure is a lack of awareness of what effective training looks like and the positive impact of implementing such training successfully.

Before the technology goes live, transformations tend to focus solely on delivering the technology, particularly when the delivery is delayed and a mountain of work is crunched up. These transformations are investing their resources and energy into building a successful system and don't have the time to think about training. We heard a good rule of thumb in one interview: "We focused 35% of [training] activities before the actual training. The actual training was 20%. 45% of training activities happened after."

In this rule of thumb, "actual" training was formal classroom-based sessions. Based on this rule of thumb, only 20% of training should be happening in a classroom. As our data show, training should not even be in a classroom but rather dedicated and protected time to learn on the job. Ideally, the remaining 80% of training activities should happen before and after the "classroom" sessions and comprise various delivery methods aside from formal classroom instruction, methods we discuss later in this chapter.

Case Study: Investing in Training

[Kim] I discussed the need to invest in training with the CFO of a midsize Danish pharmaceutical company. When I gave him a suggested estimate for how much effective training would cost, his jaw hit the floor. He told me firmly, "No way are we spending that much on training!"

My counter was "Well, you're spending far more on implementing the technology? Do you want people to use it?" It is easy to assume that technology should be intuitive, and if you send out an email, people will work it out; however, a complex technological solution is not a new iPhone. Training must be accounted for if you want end users to use the solution correctly and effectively.

Case Study: Consequences of Neglecting Training

[Kim] While it can be easy to focus on the technical aspect of a digital transformation over training, good training is a crucial factor in a transformation's success. Refraining from investing the time and effort in proper training often results in higher costs farther along the line.

A factory digitized its processes but did not invest in ensuring that the training helped end users actually use the systems once the transformation had gone live. The only training offered was the software vendor's basic "click here for this" training.

As a consequence, when the systems went live, production almost stopped. After a while – because users weren't getting spare parts for the machinery and production planning was not going as expected – people started abandoning the new system and reverting to the old spreadsheets.

After this bad first experience, the company rethought its approach. Instead of learning "which button to press," people needed to learn a new way of working. The transformation invested heavily in better training – building a 3D simulation of the entire factory to simulate the new workflows. Based on the new data, transformation leaders identified the problems and, together with management, were able to salvage the transformation.

Simulating the workflow and experience of the new systems allowed end users to have experiential and problem-based training. This training was far more valuable to end users as it provided practical experience in operating the new systems without affecting productivity.

What Is Effective Training?

There is a consistent belief that "training needs to be face to face, intensive, and meticulously taught." However, think back. How many times in your life have you sat in a classroom for three days, being lectured on a specific topic? After those three days, how successfully could you recall and retain the information you had been sitting through?

Our data showed that effective training shares certain fundamental principles. Training is structured in a varied way, taking advantage of multiple instructional channels.

Good training is designed in an engaging way (and that is not a multiple-choice quiz), allows end users to make practical use of the knowledge they are learning, and gives users an extensive amount of time to process what they are learning.

Taking Adult Learning Styles into Account

We often think of training as going back to school, sitting in a classroom practicing a particular skill in a controlled environment under the supervision of the expert who has the answers. Nothing could be further from the truth. This style of learning works with neither children nor adults.[1]

So, what do educational psychologists tell us? Classic learning through practiced repetition works for acquiring facts and perceptual skills and building muscle memory.[2] That's how we all learned to drive a car or ride a bike.

However, more is needed in most complex digital and technology change programs. As one of our interviewees said, "Training is not just about the keystrokes of the new system." This finding links directly to the benefits and impact intended for the change.

If the system's key benefits are better end-to-end process execution, the training needs to focus on the whole process – not just the keystrokes along the process but understanding the why, how, and what of the whole process.

If the change's benefits are improved data-driven decision making, better collaboration, better integration, or similar, the training must focus on understanding the operational day-to-day work required to enable those broad benefits. Often we ask users to do more – for example, enter data differently to allow better analytics; however, without understanding the wider systems and why we ask users to do more, the benefits are unlikely to materialize.

In our data, we find that nearly all training covered the aspects of using the system and changes in processes. Fewer training sessions focused on mindset and changes in roles – the latter because often roles did not change. Only about a third of training included new competencies (Figure 9.1).

In the data, we found no statistically significant difference between the training's content and its overall effectiveness. We also found no statistically significant difference between the number of different topics covered and its overall effectiveness. Our key conclusion here is that the training provided must fit the needs of organizational and technological changes.

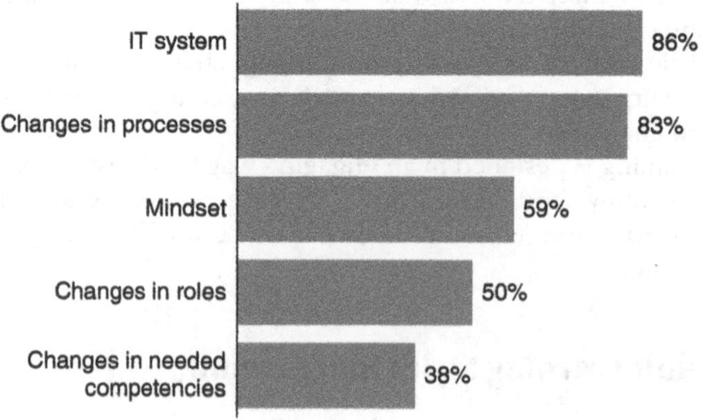

FIGURE 9.1 Focus of trainings.

Varied Delivery Methods

In our modern world, there are many more options available for training than lecturing in a classroom. While there are uses and benefits to formal classroom delivery, it is not a solution that meets every need or requirement. An effective training delivery should ideally blend several different styles of delivery, such as classroom-based training, one-to-one training, eLearning, quick how-to guides, webinars, and prototype-based training.

Our data show that training activities that relied on only one format had below-average training effectiveness. If the activities relied on two or three different formats, they were about average, and training activities that used four or more different formats were statistically significantly more effective than those with fewer formats.

At the same time, we found no statistically significant differences in our data between different formats – whether the training offered uses classic, classroom-based training, one-to-one training, eLearning, quick how-to guides, webinars, or prototype-based training. The data tell us that it is the mix and variety that makes the training effective.

The primary benefit of classroom delivery is having an expert available as well as peers experiencing the same learning process. A variety of learning delivery methods is important because it allows learners to make the most of their classroom learning time. Some information, such as learning how to log into the system, could be handled easily through eLearning or a guide, freeing up classroom time for difficult questions.

Learn About the Changes Practically

When implementing a digital transformation, the processes that need to be followed often are dramatically different from what end users have been used to. An untrained end user will find using the new systems and processes stressful. Thus, users must have encountered and familiarized themselves with the new system before it goes live.

The way to familiarize users with the changes is to simulate the processes and systems that they will be using as part of the training process. Classroom instruction, guides, and videos online are insufficient for this, as they lack the practical aspect – few processes will require you to sit and passively listen in a classroom.

Going back to the principles of good learning design, we find two frameworks handy: The first focuses on the learning objectives, and the second focuses on the instructional design.

Learning Objectives

In the first framework, you set out your learning objectives and design the training to fulfill those objectives. Bloom's taxonomy of learning – shown in Figure 9.2 – is particularly useful for guiding your thinking about learning objectives.

Imagine we want to train users how to solve a problem – say we implemented a new system for dealing with purchases. At the most basic level, we need users to *remember* how to raise a purchase order and buy something they need. But that is only the beginning; if the training covers just the bottom of Bloom's taxonomy, users will be ill-equipped to deal with issues and complex cases they might have when working with the system.

Thus, we need to include more complex problems, such as helping users *understand* different purchase orders and ways of making purchases. Good training teaches them how to *apply* their knowledge to different types of problems, such as executing purchase orders and *analyzing* a complex purchasing transaction.

If we want to equip users to do more than merely execute those skills, we also need to teach them how to *evaluate* how well the process works so they can try different ways and find better practices. If we do this well, we want them to *create* even better ways than we had envisioned initially.

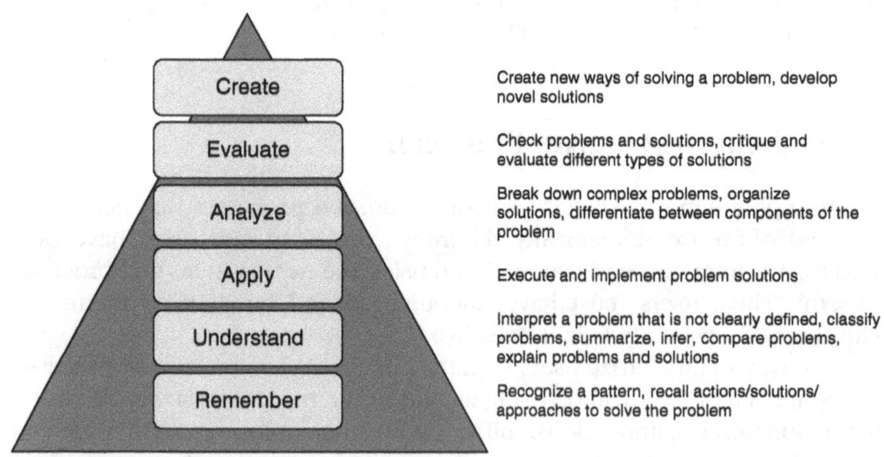

FIGURE 9.2 Bloom's taxonomy of learning.
Source: Adapted from D. R. Krathwohl, 2002. A revision of Blooms taxonomy: An overview. *Theory Into Practice*, *41*(4), 212–218.

Instructional Design

The second framework to consider is instructional design.[3] Adult learning works best when students are presented with a problem. The instructional design has three stages: Define the problem, search for an answer, and finally apply it.

In the first stage, learners need to define the problem to understand it. They build a mental model of the problem to be solved, considering what they know and don't know.

In the second stage, learners search for solutions. In their minds they evaluate whether a found solution is likely to solve the problem.

In the third stage, they apply the solution, monitor the outcomes, and vary how they apply the solution they found.

Finally, the loop goes back. Whether the possible solution is applied successfully or unsuccessfully, learners update their search process and evaluation criteria for choosing a potential solution. They also loop back to update their understanding of the problem. The key to making the learning stick is to emphasize the loops back. Make learners externalize the updates to their search and their problem definition.

If you apply this process to our purchase order training, the more appropriate training flow would be to present students with a complex purchase order. Users then access resources like FAQs, help files, or how-to guides to figure out how to raise the purchase order and execute it to see if it worked. If it does not, they start again. At the end, they discuss and reflect on who found the most elegant solution.

This framework works best when students are presented with the problem rather than the solution. If you show your students how to do something and then have them replicate the solution, students can deal only with problems that fit the exact category.

In effect, this replication method teaches them to execute a task that could have been automated in the system. We need users to deal with more complex issues, and this kind of training would not teach them how to help themselves in the future.

Acting out the process with all the elements users will encounter or need to deal with when the system is live is far more beneficial. Group sessions afterward should discuss dilemmas and analyze what worked well or failed. Information such as which button to press is more usefully included in a user manual or other similar resource that can be referred to for support when needed.

The act of building and interacting with a practical narrative is more engaging and memorable than being presented with the solution or bullet points of information when learning. Humans remember experiences more than isolated data and facts. They also remember events that inspire emotions.

Design training to provoke emotions. For example, the satisfaction learners feel when solving a complex problem is tremendously rewarding.

Other approaches help create this experiential learning, including gamifying learning or otherwise making it fun or letting users safely experience what it feels like when things go wrong.

Case Study: Training with Escape Rooms

[Alex] In our research, we interviewed the leader of a digital transformation at an engineering consultancy. The transformation took a remarkably ingenious and creative approach to making training more engaging and giving end users a chance to simulate the processes in action. The consultancy escaped the classroom by designing their training as escape rooms.

The organization had digitized all of its processes for putting together bids and so on. As this was a significant degree of change – completely changing tools, processes, and interactions – executives knew they needed to invest in making the training effective.

To do this, they designed a series of escape rooms – each one aligning to and simulating in some way a major process milestone end users would need to be familiar with in the new way of working. They then sent teams in to try to find the "solution" to each room, testing their understanding of the new systems in a gamified sandbox.

For example, one room was to get through the committee that scrutinizes whether the company would bid for a specific opportunity – something they called a black hat meeting. Teams would go in and hunt for clues and information that allowed them to put together a proposal that was up to date with the new systems and processes.

Not only was this training practical, it was also a fun team-building experience for the people going through it. Learning is far more effective when it is about more than just memorizing information. Inspiring positive emotions by making the experience fun and being there with coworkers dramatically enhances the learning experience.

Case Study: Acting Out the Scenario

[Alex] Another example of building a narrative and engaging feelings (while also eliminating boring PowerPoint presentations in a classroom approach) has yielded impressive results for a UK-based construction company.

Rather than implementing a digital transformation, the company wanted to transform its culture and approach to health and safety.

The company hired actors to stage a performance and engage with employees as part of an immersive training experience. These actors performed four scenes while interacting with the groups undergoing the training.

Scene 1: *(The construction site, December 24th.)* A foreign worker is working on the construction site. He is exhausted – he needs to work two jobs to make ends meet, and he is on his second shift today. He breaks protocol and cuts a corner a bit to save time and energy. Tragedy strikes, a workplace accident ensues, and the man dies on Christmas Eve.

Scene 2: *(Construction site boardroom, same night.)* It is chaos in the boardroom. An emergency meeting has been called due to the incident. Everyone is discussing what happened, why, and what went wrong.

Scene 3: *(Police station interrogation room, same night.)* A man is dead on company premises, and now the police are involved. You are a witness to a deadly accident. A police officer politely but insistently questions you to discover what you know. Was there anything you could have done?

Scene 4: *(A modest family home, 18 years later.)* A girl about 18 or 19 talks to you about her childhood. Her mother had tried her best to provide for her, but it had not been easy – her father had died when she was just a baby, leaving her mother to manage in a strange country by herself. A photo of the man who died on the construction site sits on the table by a Christmas tree.

After these gut-wrenching scenes, it's time for lunch and for employees to digest what they have seen. After lunch, they are allowed to go through the same scenario again. However, this time, the group can propose changes to the first scene, allowing them to try to prevent the accident.

Participants successfully prevent the accident – ensuring that the worker survives and his life is saved – and the following scenes all change. The second scene is now the Christmas party, not a crisis meeting. The third scene is removed entirely – with no accident, there is no need for the police. The fourth scene is now of a happy family quietly enjoying a lovely Christmas together.

At the end of it all, the project chief executive or chief operating officer meets everybody personally to shake their hand. At the same time,

(continued)

(continued)

the executive gives everyone the same instruction: "Do it safely or not at all. If anyone tells you to do something unsafely or cut corners, here is my telephone number and business card. Stop what you are doing immediately and call me!"

This is an enormous construction site – over 6,000 people have gone through this training. The power of this emotional narrative is self-evident; this construction project has one of the lowest accident rates in the United Kingdom.

Designing the Training

Earlier we discussed that, good training design starts with defining the learning objectives and the training content. Ideally, training should also be experiential and problem-based.

We want users to learn how to help themselves do their best at work.

When it comes to finding and creating training resources, users usually have many different options and sources of support available. Implementation consultants and software vendors often have experience with new technology and have materials and guides to create a library that users can explore to solve their problems.

During COVID-19, education shifted heavily toward digital delivery methods by necessity, accelerating a process that had already been in motion. In the future, a blended approach using digital and in-person channels will be used to deliver training. For this reason, an increasing volume of digital materials will be available to add to your library for users.

However, there is a trap here that we and our colleagues have fallen into: telling ourselves "Let's make videos to digitize training!" We learned the most important lesson: People can still read!

What do we mean by this? Learning platforms like LinkedIn Learning, YouTube, and others focus on beautifully produced video content; where is the problem?

- Creating a video is far more time-consuming than writing the same information as a written text.
- Information in videos is far more challenging to access and refer to. Content progresses linearly at a set speed, and videos make jumping around to review a specific point difficult.
- People consume information faster by reading than by listening. The average adult reads at roughly 238 words per minute,[4] while the rate of an average English speaker is about 150 words per minute.[5]

We have learned to remember that people can still read. Written text might feel less high tech than videos, but it works well. That said, there is still a place for video as a learning resource. However, if you do use videos, keep them short – our iron rule is a maximum of three minutes – and do not be afraid to supplement them with a written transcript for reference.

Finally, our data show a clear pattern for training effectiveness. Involving end users in co-planning and co-creating the training is a powerful tool for building effective training. Engaging with end users makes it easier to develop a plan and content for training that directly meets users' needs and addresses their concerns with the new systems.

According to our data, in addition to end user involvement in codesigning the training, the only instructional channel with a statistically significant link to transformation success is when frontline management prepares end users. Therefore, all training programs also need to train the trainers – frontline management must lead the training and communicate to end users about the changes.

Finally, during our interviews, we were reminded that transformations always need to remember to train the IT support staff. They do a lot of user training daily, even if they aren't officially called trainers (Figure 9.3).

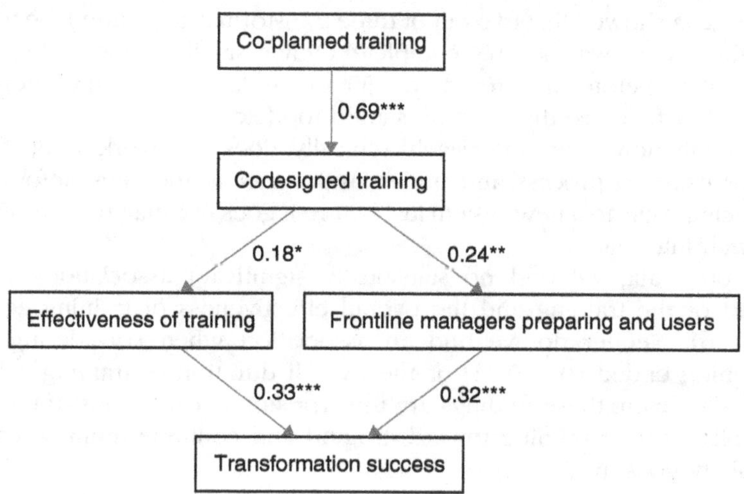

FIGURE 9.3 Explanatory variables of training effectiveness and the relation to transformation success. The figure shows only coefficients of statistically significant paths. Stars indicate statistical significance: *** p ≤ 0.001, ** p ≤ 0.01, * p ≤ 0.05.

Is Training Better over a Short or an Extended Period?

After the training is designed, the question turns to the best approach to timing. In our interviews, we encountered two typical training strategies: "short and big" and "long and small."

Few transformations followed the "short and big" approach of training all relevant users in one go – often thousands of users and typically around the go-live date. The second approach was more common. Rather than one massive burst of training over a short time, this "long and small" approach stretches the training out over a long period, with each training session focusing on specific user groups and skills.

A project that digitized how city parking is paid followed a typical training strategy. This project first launched an online training course for all users. The next stage was to go live with a pilot site where parking was now all digital. Then, using the pilot site, the first targets were the multiplicators in the organization: superusers, support desk, and middle management. Then frontline management and end users were trained. In the final phase, the users got one-to-one training.

In another project involving a central enterprise resource planning system replacement in a consultancy, the users were trained in a short session every week.

Our data showed that two out of three transformations started the training when the project was 60–70% complete. Only a small number (17%) began training at or before the project was 50% complete. Yet, in the interviews, most leaders reflected that training started too late.

Training new users intensively typically does not work well; it takes time for users to process and understand correctly the latest information. Introducing users to a new system just before it goes live may risk overloading them with information.

In our data, we find no statistically significant association between the start of the training and the overall effectiveness of training activities ($p = 0.46$). Neither do we find an association when considering when the training ended ($p = 0.44$) or the overall duration of training activities ($p = 0.84$). Again, these findings are unsurprising because most transformations roll out their training toward the end and continue training after the technology goes live.

However, we encountered a few transformations that began training earlier than the midpoint of the project's life cycle – only three out of our 155 projects started so early. Hence, our data are inconclusive in testing our question of "short and big" versus "long and small" statistically.

These three transformations were all very, very successful, however. As a result, we generally recommend beginning training as early as possible.

The AGES model inspires one approach we have used successfully.[6] The model emphasizes the role of attention, generation, emotions, and spacing in training.

- *Attention* means that during the training, participants are not distracted. Training design needs to create a space where learners can pay undivided attention.
- *Generation* is the element of training where new information is contextualized and linked to existing knowledge and other areas. Good training builds a web of learning with interconnectivity between subjects.
- *Emotions* are all about creating positive emotions for the training. Learners who approach training with fear or are forced to attend training likely will not learn. Thus, good training is needed to create positive emotions.
- *Spacing* is an essential element of learning. Single-point learning does not work. Training needs to be designed around slow learning and fast forgetting. Another crucial element is that simply repeating the same content does not result in learning. Well-designed and spaced-out training builds layers of learning.[7]

The best spacing approach starts with a fundamental exposure and then builds up. Start months in advance by introducing end users to the basics of the system, such as system logic and vocabulary. Over time, good training builds up the content, slowly moving to more complicated concepts as end users familiarize themselves with the more specific interactions with their role.

In some transformations, it is appropriate to have a brief intensive training before going live. When end users become more familiar with the topic, training can focus more on finishing polishes than starting from zero.

Interestingly, we find that this approach is less time-consuming for employees. In one specific transformation, a client we worked with estimated the hours required for an intensive classroom training approach. After following our recommendation to take an extensive, mixed-delivery approach, the client discovered that the training time required was 45% of what had been estimated using a classroom-only approach.

One reason transformations that start training earlier are less common is the fear of exposing end users to an unfinished product or system. However, even if the system is not the same as the system that will go live, there is value in end users interacting with the system and processes at all stages.

As described in Chapter 8, we found in our interviews that training is a crucial channel through which transformations can listen to the end users. Our data show that we should consider training as another type of testing. Interacting with the system as it develops allows end users to help the transformation ensure that the systems and processes fit their needs. It also encourages trust and open communication.

Having users engage with prototyping can also directly support later stages of training. By training a small group of end users to use the prototype, you are also prototyping the training. Based on data and user feedback, you can analyze and test what is or is not effective in the training and deliver a better training experience later on.

You also develop a pool of end users who are deeply experienced with the systems. These users can operate as a resource for informal training. These in-house "superusers" are available to support less experienced end users through specific questions and doubts.

Informal Training

It is essential to realize that learning does not end with going live. It can be easy to think you should load people up with the information, go live, and not worry about training. In truth, end users will have questions and will require support on an ongoing basis.

Once a technology goes live, tricky problems arise that no one thought about when designing the training. Once a system is used, users will find new ways to do their work – as one interviewee described it, "Don't forget to train and retrain!"

For this reason, frontline managers' involvement is amazingly impactful. Frontline managers who are equipped and, if needed, coached to train users (before and after going live) are a valuable resource to end users and the organization.

Frontline managers make such great trainers for several reasons:

- An established relationship exists between frontline managers and end users, making these managers trusted instructors.
- Their position as frontline managers makes them deeply familiar with the work, working environment, and teams. For this reason, they will understand how to best angle and present the training.
- Their intermediary position between the organization and end users means they will be among the first to hear and recognize when the training is going differently than planned or expected.

Case Study: Failed Training Leading to Company-wide Strikes

[Alex] Failing to invest in proper training can lead to dramatic and unforeseen consequences. An example is a bank's attempt to modernize its human resources systems. The transformation replaced existing systems with a new cloud application. Self-service by users became the new default for HR administration, replacing the old standard of contacting the HR department via email.

The data from HR are critical to running the bank. The data document absences, leave, and sick leave and determine how much people get paid. For this reason, this project faced several tremendous challenges regarding business logic, how HR rules apply in a global organization, and converting the data. The focus during the delivery was the organizational implementation and technical issues, not the usability of the software or preparing end users to use the new systems.

As a result, when the software went live, everybody in the bank found it extremely unusable and were deeply confused about how to use the software to do what they needed to do with it.

The first issue was that the system had severe usability problems. It was not well designed to be intuitive for end users, which meant it didn't address their specific needs – usability was probably one of those unspoken requirements we discussed in Chapter 6. The more significant problem, however, was the lack of attention to training. The only training provided were standard PDF tutorials from the vendor and utterly baffling videos. No other preparation took place.

End users were presented with a vital system that did not fit their needs and had not been adequately explained. As a result, all bank employees went on strike. Sixty thousand employees collectively decided the system was so poorly done that they would boycott it.

However, this system generated data vital to many other HR systems, including payroll. Moreover, the debacle created a reputational problem for the HR function.

Fixing the system exceeded the original project cost several times over. The fix rectified the usability and functionality issues. End users also were better trained on using the new systems beyond the standard tutorials and videos.

Final Recommendations

To sum up, effective training is vital to a successful implementation; if your users don't understand the new systems and processes, they won't be able to do their work. The following factors are the most influential in making training effective:

- *A varied mixed-delivery model.* Do not rely on just one channel of training delivery. A varied approach – particularly one that takes advantage of modern technology through eLearning and provides practical experience through sandboxes that provide self-training or simulations of the live experience – is more effective than classroom training alone.
- *An extensive training period.* Start as early as possible; a more extended training period allows information to be assimilated more effectively. Providing this training as early as possible – even if users are trained on an unfinished prototype – enables the training to be as effective as possible.
- *Organizational involvement.* Have frontline managers provide informal training, and end users – including the people affected by the procedures and changes within the organization – support the training's design. This approach will allow the training to best fit end users' needs.

CHAPTER 10

Lever #7: Establishing Trust-Based Relationships

Trust is important for several reasons. The large body of research into psychological safety[1] says workplaces must be emotionally, behaviorally, and cognitively safe spaces. Such spaces create an open and collaborative environment where people can openly and honestly talk about what they do or don't like, building learning and self-improving organizations. As transformation leaders, we enable productive conversations when people feel safe challenging the changes and how we deliver them.

One project manager described this situation:

It is hard as a project leader to determine the mood on the ground. When we did this project [an extensive change to all systems related to pay in a multinational consumer goods company], the supplier had most of the development team in India. The project was under immense time pressure, and we needed an organization that flagged issues much faster to resolve them faster.

We needed to create more transparency and trust with our suppliers. I listened in on their weekly status calls to get a better picture of what was going on. I noticed that when everything went well, many people spoke. If something wasn't going to plan, only the seniors spoke.

Another perspective is that without trust, you are forced into micromanagement. If managers do not trust their teams or do not inspire trust, micromanagement is needed to maintain control over the project or to feel confident that things are on track. In the real world, this approach is not approach.

As leaders, we have multiple relationships where we need to build trust. The most important relationship is with our teams. The organizational psychologists Steven Brown and Thomas Leigh identified the factors that create a favorable psychological climate at work, which enables greater employee involvement in the work and determines the effort level of employees.[2]

Brown and Leigh identified the factors that must be present for employees to "walk the extra mile." The two critical elements of a productive workplace climate are psychological safety and the psychological meaningfulness of work.

The freedom of self-expression,[3] supportive management, and clarity of expectations create psychological safety. Making a clear contribution, recognition for their work, and having a level of challenge make work meaningful.

The research of Amy Edmondson, professor of leadership at Harvard Business School, identifies leaders' behaviors that build psychological safety and enable learning teams. Leaders need to:

- Frame the work as a learning problem or experiment, not an execution problem
- Acknowledge limits/own fallibility
- Embrace messengers of tough issues and ideas
- Model curiosity and ask lots of questions and
- Encourage dissent.

Trust needs to be built in two further directions: upward with senior stakeholders and downward with end users, who must eventually use the implemented solution. If trust is not inspired in either or both groups, problems will arise.

In both cases, it is important to build a relationship of trust. Doing so allows you to share bad news and talk about tough issues productively while solving problems together. It also helps both groups stay aligned with the project. When groups are aligned, it becomes easier for both stakeholders and end users to see the transformation as a mutual benefit rather than a zero-sum game in which one side wins and the other loses.

We touched upon the issue of trust in the discussion of effective communication in Chapter 8. We found statistically significant differences between trust in the project delivering the transformation and the person perceived to be the key communicator about the changes. This finding serves as a reminder that trust is fundamentally a person-to-person phenomenon.

Stakeholder trust is vital. Studies demonstrating the need for such trust include Chris Sauer's research on the failure of IT projects.[4] The first issue Sauer's research uncovered was that no project was an outright success or failure. In his case studies, few people thought that a delayed go-live or a cost overrun means the project failed.

In the end, he found that there is only one characteristic on which everyone agrees that a project is a failure: when it is abandoned before finishing. His research then uncovered a common pattern: Projects are never abandoned because of a technical problem. Projects get abandoned only when stakeholders lose trust in them.

Trust between clients and contractors, vendors, and suppliers is equally important to simplify the governance of contracts. Higher levels of trust reduce transaction and governance costs.[5] Moreover, trust between contractual parties in a project is necessary for knowledge transfer. Trust improves quality management and is necessary for high-performance integrated project teams.[6]

Trust in the vendor-client relationship has been well studied. Vendors are trusted if they are reliable, open, and honest. Studies of system implementation failures have argued that failures might be due to a lack of ability to carry out system customization and a lack of caring. Some vendors might genuinely not want to help their clients, might lack honesty by hiding problems, or a combination.[7]

Equally, projects need to establish trust with end users. Such trust is built through credibility that demonstrates that you have the experience and authority to implement beneficial change. The literature we reviewed clearly connects trust and system adoption in the case of e-government projects.

End users need to trust a system to enter sensitive information – for example, electronic medical records, filing taxes online, signing up for online banking, or buying consumer goods with credit cards. Research has found that when users trust a system, they perceive risks to be lower, and lower risk perception is directly linked to system usage.[8]

In the case of enterprise software, users do not necessarily have to trust the system or the project. They are provided with a new tool to do their work, and they need to use the tool to continue to be employed by the company. Unfortunately, we found no research looking into the role of trust in the adoption of internal systems.

The data we collected in our research fills this gap. We find a clear and statistically significant association between the degree of trust with end users and stakeholders and achieving the intended impact, adoption of the system, and overall transformation success (Figure 10.1).

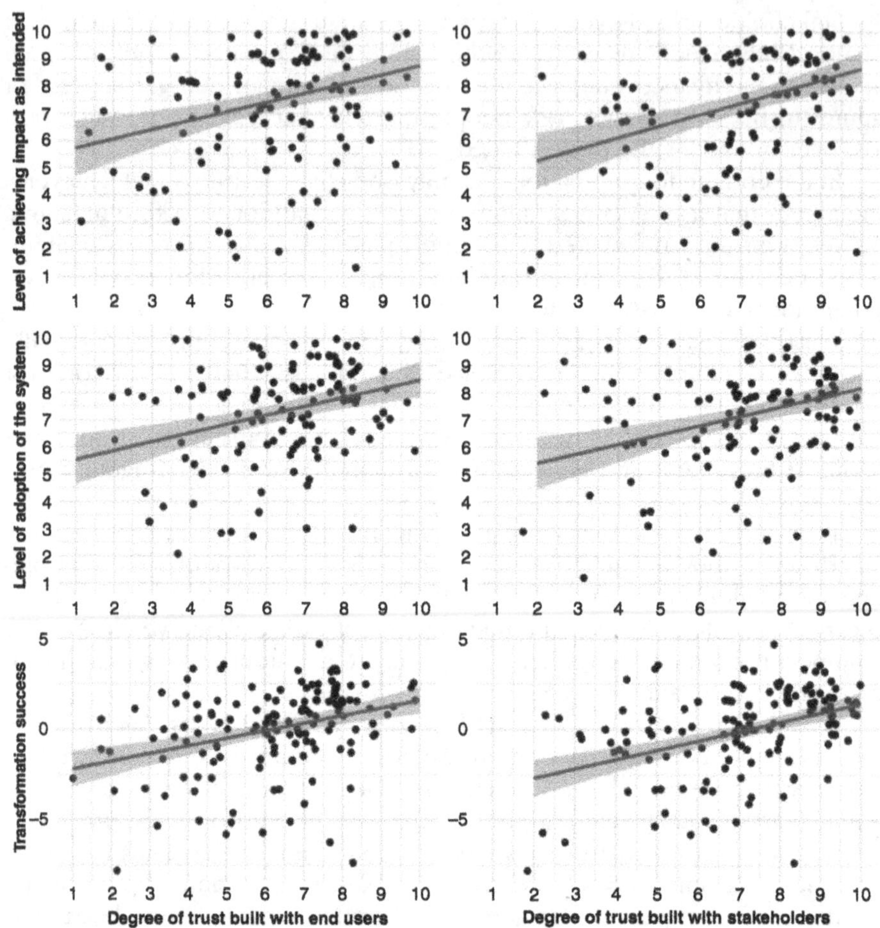

FIGURE 10.1 Linear relationship between the degree of trust built with end users and stakeholders and the digital transformation outcomes in terms of system adoption, achievement of impact as intended, and overall transformation success. (All linear relationships are statistically significant.) Linear regressions: End user and stakeholder trust associated with intended impact (BF = 93, BF = 2570), adoption of the system (BF = 455, BF = 395), and transformation success (BF = 678, BF =17999). Post hoc equivalent did not show any statistically significant differences between the effect strengths of trust with end users compared to trust with stakeholders (impact BF = 3.1, adoption BF = 1, transformation success BF = 3.5).

The issue with building and sustaining trust is that trust is intangible. This fact came up repeatedly in our research; change leaders were aware that building trust with stakeholders and end users was important, but they found it hard to know how to create trust. One of our research questions then was to analyze who and what in organizations implementing changes had a measurable impact on building trust.

One thing that we have learned was surprising. Change leaders are often good at creating trust upward in their organizational structures or toward the stakeholders; however, they struggle with building trust with end users – who are equally crucial for the transformation to succeed. In our data, we found that established stakeholder trust levels are statistically significantly higher than end user trust ($p < 0.001$).

In the data, we found that only half the projects had established high levels of trust with both end users and stakeholders. A little more than one in four projects had high levels of trust with stakeholders but only low levels of trust with end users, and nearly one in four had low levels of trust with either (Table 10.1).

TABLE 10.1 Trust-based relationships with end users and stakeholders in the data.

	Low trust with stakeholders	High trust with stakeholders
Low trust with end users	21%	26%
High trust with end users	7%	46%

Logically, it makes sense that leaders are better at gaining the steering committee's trust than end users' trust. To begin with, there are fewer members of the steering committee. A steering committee often has 10 or so people in a boardroom. Moreover, as the steering committee members are the ones who are giving the money and helping, it is natural that leaders of transformations spend time with them and build a better relationship.

It is far easier to walk into the CEO's office and discuss the transformation's progress to get that person's perspective. End users, in contrast, might number in the thousands and be spread over the globe, with wildly different needs and issues.

If you implement an IT system and users don't trust it or trust you when you tell them it is necessary, they won't use it.

Case Study: No Trust Between Headquarters and Local Branches

[Alex] We worked in an Eastern European bank to establish a shared service center for back-office operations. Our team was hired by the owner of a large European retail bank that owned various regional banks. The business case was clear: A shared service center for functions like payroll or commercial banking products like bond origination made sense when we sat in the bank's head office.

I was met with visceral rejection of this idea when I visited the local head offices to discuss it. No one in the regional banks trusted the headquarters or the other regional banks. Each was convinced that its neighbors could not possibly pay employees correctly.

In one of the offices, I heard a funny story of how deep the mistrust runs. A few years earlier, the main headquarters decided to roll out a collateral management system for all subsidiary banks. A collateral management system keeps track of all the securities given to the bank in return for a mortgage or a loan; for example, the house that is mortgaged or the car that a car loan is financing. The system was a well-known software product by an EU vendor. The IT staff in this Eastern European branch saw the need but thought the costs were astronomical.

Unfortunately, there was minimal trust between this branch and its head office. The local executives saw doing what they were told and buying from the EU vendor as a waste of money and resources and were not inclined to trust that the cost was even necessary. Why pay so much when a local developer charges a fraction for a day's work compared to the European vendor?

So, they sent one of their developers to look at a reference installation. The developer returned, and within four weeks, the branch had reengineered the solution entirely – they even put the same vendor logo into the system.

The local branch's team then returned to headquarters to tell them that, as requested, they were now using the system, which cost less than €10,000 to build. Headquarters was furious and told the branch's team they would be charged the full anticipated cost for rolling out and running the system anyway; it was up to them to stick with their own pirated system or use the real system. The local bank caved in and switched.

We never set up a shared service center – even though it took us nearly four months to convince the head office that the project would never work because of the underlying trust issues.

While the change might make sense to the organization, it might represent more effort and inconvenience to end users, who need help seeing how or why they should fully embrace it. The payback for the change might be at the organizational level, not for day-to-day end users. To adopt these innovations, users must trust the transformation when it explains the rationale.

Imagine a pharmacy updating its systems and requiring more data about someone collecting a prescription – perhaps to prevent two individuals with the same name from being given the wrong medicine. The system's end user – the employee handing out the prescriptions – might go from just entering the customer's name and that of the medication to needing to collect and record the address, phone number, and date of birth.

The organization benefits from increased security by avoiding medication errors and preventing potentially costly liabilities. End users, however, now have to collect, confirm, and enter far more data. They also need to learn how to use the new system correctly *and* handle customers complaining that filling prescriptions is now a longer and more complicated process.

These end users might feel that they are expected to do more for no real reason other than "it's good for the organization." To realize the full benefits of the transformation, end users need to trust that the promised benefits will arise, and they need to trust their leaders when they say that the transformation is necessary.

Equally, even when end users directly benefit from the system, trust is necessary. During our interviews, we repeatedly heard that trust was low when the project started – too many transformations had happened that made promises they never delivered.

According to our data, which we analyzed in Chapter 4, building and rebuilding trust was a pivotal precursor to the success of all transformations. This is true not only because a transformation asks users to do extra work by engaging with the project in workshops, meetings, and the like in addition to their usual workloads but also because users are asked to innovate and contribute their knowledge and insights.

Imagine that some change consultant you have never met before comes to your desk and wants to understand the pain points in a process you are responsible for. No one wants to look bad in their job. Trust is necessary for you to share meaningful insights.

> ## Case Study: Engaging More with End Users
>
> [Tom] The end users did not mean much to me. I thought all that was needed was for them to turn up and work their assigned shift and duties as required. At that time, I believed that, for the people in my team to deliver what they needed on time, I had to be strict and act as a direct authority over the team.
>
> I now see that there are better approaches than this. Historically, the industry just recently learned of the value of trust. Now we recognize that a professional, skills-based approach to building trust is needed.
>
> Users need to use the system to generate the benefits of a transformation. Therefore, establishing an informal trust base is the first step to delivering benefits. By contrast, the steering committee might be more interested in the issues and problem-solving aspects. These are two very different worlds that we are combining into one skill set.

How Is Trust Built?

Change management believes that "Trust is built by credibility and if people are delivering reliably." We believe this is true, but there is more to trust than credibility and reliability. Otherwise, all that would be required would be regular update emails from a suitably believable source with an impressive email signature.

Our literature review found that trust in projects has been studied between organizations, such as contractual partners or members of an alliance.[9] Our research also found that people-to-people relationships are at the core of trust. You cannot build trust without paying attention to the human aspect; some form of humanity and connection must be established in the relationship.

In some instances, organizations can make up for the lack of trust in people by having employees who trust the procedural fairness and predictability of the organization. Such a situation might arise in transformations with large numbers of redundancies.[10]

Therefore, we believe that there is an interpersonal equation behind trust. David Maister, a business author and former Harvard Business School professor, first proposed the trust equation.[11] The equation was developed for consultants, who must be trusted advisors. The book's authors created a list of characteristics of trusted advisors and then synthesized it into a simple formula. According to their formula, trust is built through credibility, reliability, and intimacy, while it is destroyed through self-orientation.

- *Credibility:* *"I can trust what she says about intellectual property; she's very credible on the subject."* This is trust built by words – the credentials of a firm or a consultant. But it is not just credentials. It is also presence. How a consultant communicates credibility is essential – typically through illustration or example, not assertions.
- *Reliability:* *"If he says he'll deliver the product tomorrow, I trust him because he's dependable."* This is trust built by actions. Advisors must be dependable, behave consistently, and follow through on their intentions and promises.
- Intimacy: *"I can trust her with that information; she's never violated my confidentiality before, and she would never embarrass me."* Trust is built by emotions. It is present when we can openly discuss tricky situations and is created by psychological safety.
- *Self-orientation:* *"I can't trust him on this deal – I don't think he cares enough about me; he's focused on what he gets out of it."* This is trust destroyed by motives. Consultants do not get promoted by clients. Thus, if trust is to be built, we need to be sure that our advisors' motives align with our objectives and that we share a common goal.

While trust is generally intangible, focusing on directly observable behaviors is a valuable way to make trust more tangible. As previously stated, conversations without practical action or results must be avoided. Accordingly, we found that in an environment that lacks trust, reporting and templates would not result in discussions revolving around solutions. Meanwhile, in a trusting environment, progress often happens directly from conversations.

In our data, we find that the consequences of trust are not only the achieved impact and system adoption, as described earlier, but also higher levels of trust with stakeholders and end users that increase the ease of accessing and acquiring resources needed, such as experts, people, time, and money. Higher levels of trust also generate a more positive attitude toward the project and the change. Although only trust by end users is linked to a more positive attitude – that is, commitment toward the change – stakeholder trust is not statistically significant in this case (Figure 10.2).

We hypothesized that credibility, reliability, and intimacy create trust. In our data, we do not find that reliability creates trust (Figure 10.3). This finding may be because it is assumed that projects deliver as promised – isn't that what projects are all about? We also find that credibility creates trust only with end users, not with stakeholders.

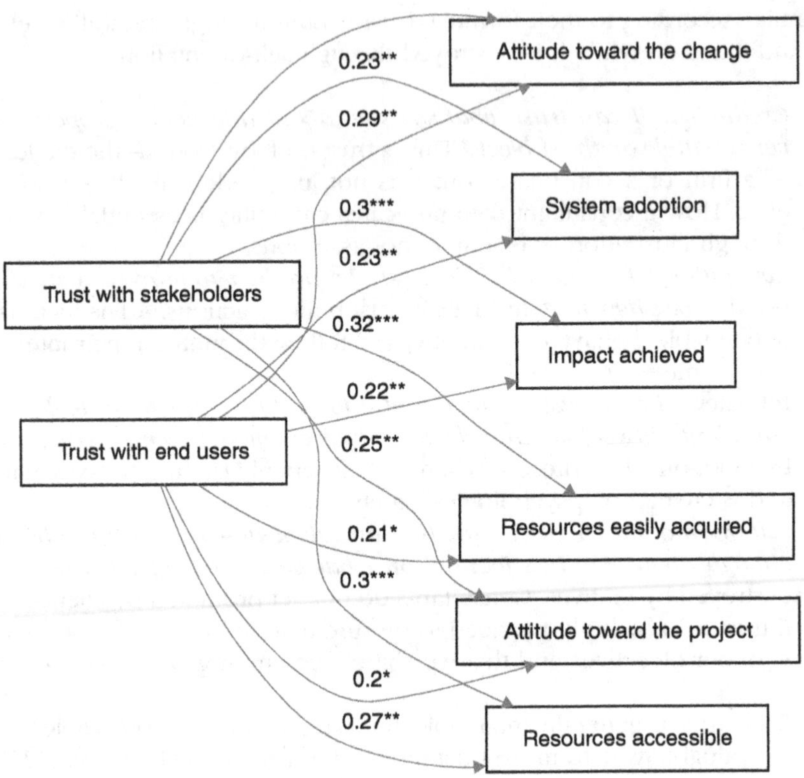

FIGURE 10.2 The consequences of high levels of trust.

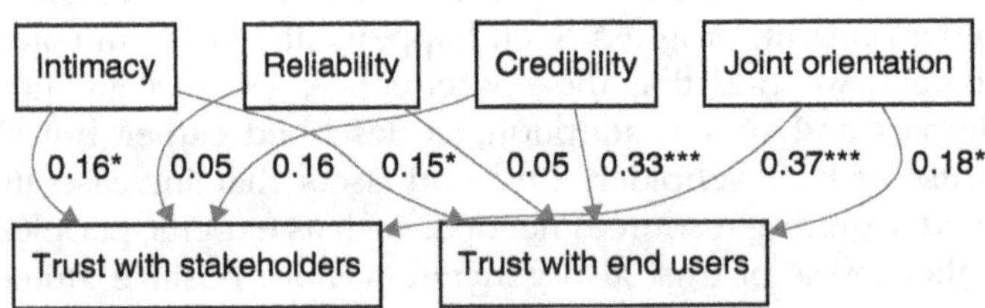

FIGURE 10.3 How trust is built. Model of the trust equation factors associated with the trust-based relationships with stakeholders and end users. The figure shows all coefficients on the paths. Stars indicate statistical significance: *** $p \leq 0.001$, ** $p \leq 0.01$, * $p \leq 0.05$. The model fitted to the data shows that stakeholder trust is statistically significantly associated with the orientation toward joint goals (effect 0.37, $p < 0.001$) and intimacy (effect 0.16, $p = 0.027$). Trust with end users is statistically significantly associated with credibility (effect 0.33, $p < 0.001$), intimacy (effect 0.15, $p = 0.046$), and joint goals (effect 0.18, $p = 0.038$).

The model also shows us that a common-goal orientation (i.e., the inverse of self-orientation) and intimacy are more impactful levers to build trust than credibility.

What trust might look like varies depending on the context. It is easy to think of trust as a one-size-fits-all thing, but our research suggests that it changes depending on the relationship. We need to consider trust between the project and stakeholders and between the project and end users.

When dealing with stakeholders, the critical factor for building trust was less about credibility and reliability and more about intimacy and orientation toward a common goal. The effect of sharing the same goals for the transformation is twice as important in building trust compared to creating intimacy with stakeholders.

When we look only at end users' trust, however, we find that credibility is the most influential creator of trust, followed by orientation toward a common goal and intimacy. Again, reliability is not a statistically significant influencer of trust.

Building Reliability, Intimacy, and Credibility on a Project-Level Basis

Often people will work to build trust on an intuitive, person-to-person basis. This work might be done by leading by example while being honest and authentic. If you make a promise or commitment, you follow through on it. You make your values and morals clear – you avoid gossiping about others or betraying any trust or confidence they have given you, for example.

However, how is trust built between a project and the group of users and stakeholders rather than between the two individuals who are the transformation leader and the CEO? The focus here needs to be on ensuring that communication and conversations are open and honest, enabling users, stakeholders, and the team leading the transformation to discuss what is not going well with the transformation.

It quickly becomes apparent that this trust mechanism is closely interlinked with two other change management levers: communication and user involvement.

Most leaders want to share achievements to inspire confidence in the transformation. In order to do this, on big projects the messaging tends to focus on their progress and to celebrate successes. However, end users and stakeholders usually know that endless celebrations are not honest – few projects run without setbacks.

Discussing setbacks and challenges builds trust and intimacy – they should not be swept under the carpet. Acknowledging when you are struggling is more authentic and creates intimacy with whoever is on the other side. Ensuring that the communication is honest and authentic makes it easier for reports of success to seem credible when they are given.

Another trap to avoid is what we referred to in Chapter 4 as a submarine-style implementation. Transformations that disappear without any communication or user interaction lack reasons for people to trust them when a project resurfaces.

In this case, there is not much trust because there is no intimacy – in fact, there is no interaction at all. It is remarkably difficult to build trust in an environment where nobody knows what is going on. Without user involvement, there can be no relationship or ability to ensure the system reliably fits end users' needs.

Case Study: Danish Building Organization

[Tom] I did a massive project for the Danish Building Organization, which builds public sector facilities, such as offices. The organization needed help implementing new IT solutions and replacing old systems with an integrated core system. Doing this involved taking a UK-based solution and making it comply with Danish legislation for the field.

By coincidence, and by putting in a lot of personal effort and time on location with top management and key stakeholders (amusingly, I had a personal connection thanks to the sponsor having worked with my father years before on a different job), I was able to create a solid and intimate relationship with management and the steering committee from the beginning.

This preexisting relationship made working together to complete the project far easier. We were able to build trust quickly, have a complete and honest dialogue, and have a trustful delivery setup. For this reason, we could admit what we were good or bad at and ask for support when needed.

The vice president felt comfortable passing the reins over to me when needed. He was terrific at delivering on the operational aspect of the organization; however, this was the first time he had done IT implementation. Our trust-based relationship meant he was comfortable asking me to help him with that – he would support me, and I could do whatever was needed.

Two years into the transformation, he admitted that IT was outside his field. He had been making decisions based on the wrong mindset because he had never worked with IT delivery before. He was surprised that I hadn't insisted more on educating him so he could have impacted the implementation positively.

We did run into quite a few problems during the project. However, his faith in us meant that he leaned in and trusted the advice from the IT delivery organization that I was heading. He had the confidence to let us solve the problem without getting involved in IT issues or getting in the way.

When we moved into the operational part of the project, which was more in his comfort zone, he stepped in and took over a bit more. In the end, we delivered on time and budget – earning a bonus for the third-party IT vendor as a result.

The success of this project hinged on our ability to share the reins smoothly. Building a trusting relationship is the trust equation at work: We started from a position of credibility because we were both in senior leadership positions in the same organization. Reliably solving IT problems fostered his trust in me, and his solving operational issues did the same for me. We also created a psychologically safe space that allowed us to cooperate and talk openly, which was crucial. And finally, we were aligned on our objectives to win together.

Fisticuffs at Midnight

[Alex] This is a true story, which might look strange but was a quirk of genius. It happened on my very first major digital transformation in an investment bank in the early 2000s. In the organization, there was deep mistrust between the investment banking division and IT.

I was hired by the head of the investment bank to investigate this strange project he did not understand. The project had already finished and introduced a middleware layer in the architecture. The head of investment banking thought that this project was why all his projects had become so much more expensive and that he would save money if his division had its own IT department.

(continued)

> *(continued)*
>
> My analysis discovered that this was not true. Projects were not more expensive, the middleware saved money, and having two IT departments would create chaos.
>
> Ready with my draft report, I went into a briefing meeting late one evening. Twenty minutes into the meeting, he stood up and left the room; I hurriedly followed. He then proceeded to the big room where the IT employees were sitting and announced that I disagreed with his hypothesis and that, being convinced of the facts, the only option left would be a boxing match. He then ran downstairs to tell the investment bankers the same.
>
> Shortly after that, we had a pretend boxing match – only comical blows were exchanged between two slightly overweight people – and we quickly hugged and left for the night.
>
> Neither of us would act in the same way in today's workplaces, but this charade very publicly and comically showed both teams that it is okay to speak up. It was the beginning of reestablishing trust, which was tremendously helpful in the turnaround of one of the flagship transformations that followed.

How Have We Used Our Research?

As a result of our research, we have learned several lessons. One of the primary insights is to focus not just on the stakeholders and steering committees. We began to spend a lot more time with end users and their managers than with upper management. While this approach is harder and more time-consuming, it has benefits. As Marshall Goldsmith, an executive coach and author, says[12]: "Leadership is a contact sport" – you can't lead via email and without investing the time for making contact.

Only by spending time with end users can you see what actually worries or concerns them, which means that you can operate smarter. Spending time with end users also helps to create their commitment to change and allows faster and more impactful implementations.

In many of the digital transformations we work on, the technology is delivered first, and then you start realizing benefits. But these benefits take quite some time to become evident.

Since we did the research, we observed that if you build trust with end users, they develop confidence in the new way of working – even if the solution is not yet fully implemented or not all functionalities are available.

Having a trust-based relationships with users allows the transformation to start realizing benefits before the delivery is complete. End users will be eager to engage with the solution and earn the benefits for the organization. They will also be able to identify whether the solution might not work for them, allowing the solution to be optimized during the process.

We have concluded a few rules of thumb for ourselves, which you might want to consider:

1. Do more listening than talking.
2. Think out loud.
3. Do not think less of yourself; think of yourself less.

Listening builds intimacy, which is valuable for building relationships with stakeholders and end users. It helps you to understand and address stakeholders' concerns, and it creates an atmosphere in which end users know they can share their concerns.

Thinking out loud enables honest communication and intimacy. As we said earlier, sharing vulnerability when things are not going perfectly builds the relationship and makes you more credible when discussing benefits and successes.

Self-orientation is the critical factor that weakens any trust-based relationship. While you should not dismiss your value and ability to contribute, the transformation impacts users and their organization the most. Their concerns and needs take priority – end users first.

Based on these precepts, we recommend an open approach to talking with your end users. The more they are involved and included in the process, the more they will see your credibility and trust that the solution fits their needs. Putting less focus on stating your credibility to deliver a transformation might seem like a subtle shift in how you approach meetings, but we have learned from this research that if we step into a user meeting feeling pressured to sell the transformation, something is wrong.

Therefore, start showing them the solution very early on. Don't be embarrassed to share something with errors, mistakes, or design problems. By seeing the project evolve and being able to share feedback on it, end users will feel more ownership and attachment to the transformation.

Of course, this approach can be scary for a transformation leader. We can be prone to an older mindset in which the transformation is built according to the design, and any defects or adjustments are collected afterward. However, we should fearlessly encourage open dialogue without having a solution ready for every issue that surfaces.

Another way we have applied our research is to scrutinize communication. As described in Chapter 8, effective communication is the primary channel to build trust, followed by trust created through emotions and behaviors. On several transformations, we have used those insights and stopped all communication reinforcing reliability– no more communications about milestones and progress. Instead, we turn those around to talk about joint goals achieved and how this results from our transformation's ability to empathize with users.

Ultimately, taking the time needed to meet and build relationships with end users is a good investment. When users trust you, they can help you see problems faster and make early adjustments to the transformation, reducing the time and money required for making changes and optimizations.

Conclusion – Designing Better Transformations

Managing organizational change is an important and indispensable part of any digital transformation. Our extensive combined experience and joint research have never left us any doubt about this. We did not expect the process of researching and writing this book to change our approaches to transformations, the extent by which we advanced our effectiveness as professionals, or the advice we give to others managing their transformations.

Sharing Our Discoveries

A common problem with change management is that often it is a bit of a black box. Business leaders might know that a successful transformation includes a change management team, but they don't understand why it is essential. The result is a transformation where change is not appropriately integrated into the project management processes or might even be a last-minute afterthought. Too often, we see IT-led projects that ought to be digital transformations.

Business leaders prioritize technological change over the organizational change because they have clear, measurable, and tangible benefits. Organizational change management, in contrast, historically has been a more abstract and vaguer field, particularly as the effectiveness of any one of the many frameworks available might vary dramatically between organizations or teams.

The data collected through our research are invaluable in our conversations with top management and decision makers about the value of managing change. Previously, they would have agreed that change management was important but were confused about why and what they should focus on to ensure the transformation had the most significant possible impact.

Having data and research to refer to makes the concept far more concrete and tangible. We now provide measurable data proving precisely why and how change management can help a project succeed. We can clearly communicate what exactly leaders should be doing and when. Basing our actions as leaders of digital transformations on academic and practical evidence ensures that change management is happening correctly.

How Our Approaches Have Changed

Before working on this book, we focused our efforts on the bigger picture – working on broad communication or ensuring management was on board. Then, if needed, we could step in closer to put out fires.

Our research showed that effective communication and transferring the ownership of the transformation to management are essential and should be part of managing a transformation. However, a different focus and the knowledge that we need to go deep into the tactics of some areas but not all help reduce both our effort and the number of fires we need to fight.

Getting closer to end users and to where changes happen means that we can prevent issues that could be extraordinarily disruptive and resource-demanding before they become a problem. We spend more time helping frontline managers translate the change into something tangible and relevant to end users, letting them understand how it will affect their daily lives.

The Importance of the Seven Levers

We started with seven beliefs when we conducted the research that led to this book. These beliefs came from the vast body of research on technology-led change in organizations. Hundreds of practitioners supported us in distilling and validating our starting position.

We know that digital transformations do not follow an easy recipe. There is no handbook for change. Instead, we think of transformation leaders as professionals who must make choices when faced with significant uncertainty and project fluidity. We tied each of the beliefs to the seven levers, which we consider critical factors of managing transformations – these are the seven levers that change leaders need to make choices about.

When we reviewed the literature, we saw that the published research focuses mainly on strategy and setting the organizational context – the work of top management. Often these insights come from case studies. They ring true at face value. Yet we wanted to go a level deeper. What do successful digital transformations do? How do they translate a great strategy into impact? How do they make a great strategy even better?

We put some hard science into our research over several years. As we learned more, we realized that some of these beliefs were misconceptions and that while others might be valuable advice, they might not be complete by themselves and may work in surprising ways.

Lever #1: Clear Reason for Change

Implementing change is a significant investment – no organization ever starts a transformation without carefully considering the decision. However, to manage change effectively, you must recognize that establishing a clear reason in the abstract is not enough. As the saying goes, you must lift the strategy off the page. You must actively provide a rationale for the transformation so that others commit to that change and engage with the transformation.

Two primary motivations for transformations are to fix a broken, burning platform or to pursue a positive result – the pot-of-gold narrative. However, it is important to recognize that the people you are co-opting into the change effort will not necessarily share the organization's motivations. What motivates the organization to change usually is not what motivates end users or stakeholders to accept that change.

Our data found that a polished rationale for change is counterproductive – it turns employees off. Instead, we found through our interviews that not only do employees appreciate being part of the visioning, but they also demand active co-creation.

Co-creating the rationale for change makes trust, effective communication, and management ownership of the transformation vital. For example, frontline managers – as they understand the needs of their teams – will be able to present motivations and benefits to end users much better than a CEO can.

Having been effectively targeted by a trusted spokesperson, end users will be more likely to accept the necessity of change and the ensuing inconvenience and disruption to their lives. Senior management provides focus, and their authority can cut through inertia, yet defining the rationale is the whole work of the organization, not just the top.

A clear reason for the change is excellent to have and is an element of successful transformations. However, there is more to managing change than having just one "big why." A clear, tailored rationale makes communicating the need for change more straightforward, but we now know that the perfect vision is less important than you think.

We now spend far less time on clarifying the reason for change than we did previously. Ultimately, once the reason has been clarified enough to make communicating about the change easier and to help identify and manage benefits, we believe time might be better spent on other tasks.

Lever #2: Defined Approach to Managing Change

Having a defined approach is *useful*; however, the data did not show a direct impact of such an approach on a transformation's success. Instead, we found that having a defined approach and plan for the project was useful mostly for securing resources, funding, and personnel. A defined approach also makes creating trust in the project and convincing stakeholders easier, and these things are very useful to any transformation.

While a top-down waterfall approach remains the most common approach to managing change according to our data, we didn't see anything suggesting the waterfall is particularly effective. In fact, since change management is more of a cyclical process than a linear one, as the other levers suggest, a linear waterfall approach can even cause problems.

Effective transformation management revolves around building trust and engagement by constantly taking feedback and optimizing and adjusting accordingly. For this reason, planning and structuring milestones and deliverables cannot be a fixed process; the approach needs to be flexible and allow for adjustments as the transformation progresses.

We found that it is necessary to create more feedback loops. Feedback from the grassroots of the organization needs to be continually passed up to the top. The direction and strategy flowing down from the top of the organization are, therefore, based on and informed by the feedback being passed up.

Having a defined approach makes securing resources easier, as does having a clear reason for the change. And as with the clear reason to change, investing time in developing a detailed approach is only partially necessary beyond what is needed to build trust and convince stakeholders.

Successful transformations, however, are defined by the ability to adapt to the circumstances and reality of the project. Spending too much time and effort on defining the approach risks limiting your ability to adapt or wasting time redefining the approach whenever the situation changes.

Lever #3: Early Involvement of Users

We had expected to discover that the earlier end users get involved, the better. Everyone knows that failing fast is better than failing at the user acceptance test of a system in the final months of a multiyear project.

However, we were surprised to discover that the situation is a little more complicated. User involvement *is* critical – it is a vital part of testing and making sure the solution will work. But if you involve users too early and randomly, they might not understand exactly what they are sharing feedback on or how doing so could help them.

More useful is involving the *right* users and subject matter experts in testing. Having feedback from someone who properly understands the system workflow and the intended value the organization wants to get out of the transformation can be far more valuable than having general testing feedback from an early stage. The issue is that what might sound like a good idea on paper is extremely challenging to pull off in practice.

Getting hold of the true experts in an organization is tough. They are busy. They are often involved in multiple projects. Their time is gold dust.

If the granularity of your project plan tells you that you need one day a week from an expert in the accounting department for the next three years, you run the risk of getting whoever is available.

From the data and our experience, we learned that it is important to engage with the right users, especially when things are still uncertain and up in the air. Identifying subject matter experts within your user base allows you to ensure that the feedback you are getting in the early stages directly addresses any organization-specific needs.

We learned that you must meticulously plan your use of the expert's precious time. Don't waste it by showing them slideshows or having general discussions. The best approach is to show them the thing and listen.

In other words, the earlier users become involved in testing and providing feedback, the better. Successfully managing change depends on getting actionable, high-quality feedback from two types of end users: those who know the ins and outs of daily work and those who know how their peers are affected by the change. The earlier you start letting these end users engage with the new system, the more feedback that is generated and the better the solution.

As testing progresses, you open up to the broader user base. In addition to helping keep the project in focus, these cycles of user testing allow you to start developing and optimizing your training program; using frontline managers as testers, for example, will enable you to equip them with the experience to serve as support and informal trainers later on.

Lever #4: Management Ownership

Much of the research on management ownership of change focuses heavily on the top management levels. The belief is that if the senior levels are on board, then everything else will flow from the top down. We have learned that middle and frontline managers often can benefit more from the change management team's support than top management can.

While top managers are an essential part of managing change, a transformation cannot be the problem of top management alone. Frontline managers buying into the transformation and becoming emotionally attached and invested in its success is by far the most needed element when engaging with management.

Trust and buy-in from end users are vital to success and change. The frontline managers' job is to communicate and build this trust and buy-in. Therefore, they are responsible for making sure that the transformation's benefits are realized. For this reason, it is vital that frontline managers are willing and able to own their part in this process.

Part of the role that top-level managers have to play is enforcing a culture that makes every level of management feel accountable for the results of the transformation. Top management are also vital to ensure that communication flows up and down the command chain and to ensure that the organization and its managers focus on the right things.

Yet, as we found, managers at every level often do not know what to do. They are neither change nor technology specialists. It would be best to communicate clear expectations of what you want them to do, how, and why. Then you need to support, equip, and coach them and hold them accountable.

Today, we spend far more time getting our hands dirty on the front lines of organizations than we did before – coaching frontline managers and middle managers on how to communicate and translate information about the transformation up and down the chain.

Lever #5: Effective Communication

Throughout our research, specific keywords and concepts kept coming up. "Dialogue," "targeted and relevant," and "positive reinforcement" were significant ones. An easy way to communicate with an organization is with unfocused broadcasts of information. In our experience and from our research, broadcasting messages to everyone simply does not result in effective communication. Instead, all it does is increase the level of noise, which in most organizations is high to begin with.

Too often, projects communicate for the sake of it. These general broadcasts do nothing to build end users' trust. The messages also do nothing to earn and hold attention, particularly when people might be constantly bombarded with seemingly irrelevant information.

Remember the story of the boy who cried wolf? If the last five broadcasts have nothing to do with them, people will automatically assume that the email they just received is a pointless update and irrelevant to them. If a message needs to reach your end users, delivering it through a targeted dialogue that is relevant to them makes the communication more likely to work.

Our data showed that frontline managers need to be the communicators for the most productive dialogue. Again, however, frontline managers need to be coached and supported to be effective communicators. You need to think about how to coach and support frontline managers in their efforts. Frontline managers who have the support they need to take ownership of this task will find adapting and targeting the message as required far easier.

The focus of any communication must address the needs and concerns of end users. While the impact on the organization as a whole might be of interest, end users truly need to know how *they* will be affected by the change. It will affect them most, so they need to understand what the change will look like and how they will benefit from the inconvenience. They will want to know how you intend to make the transformation a fair process and how they will be cared for throughout.

Lever #6: Effective Training

Learning face to face in instructor-led sessions is the way we remember school. Training on how to use a new system often takes the form of classroom lectures delivered days before the system goes live. This approach typically does not work very well. No one ever learned how to drive a car by looking at PowerPoint presentations.

A classroom lecture does very little to make the new information relevant, nor does it help end users practice or internalize it – a week later, they have forgotten everything and wish they could continue using the systems they are familiar with already. While face-to-face sessions continue to be an important part of training, they need to be applied correctly and with purpose.

For training to be effective, end users need to practice and experience the information they need to know as part of an ongoing and iterative training process. In addition, the more relevant the information is to their specific needs, roles, and workflow, the better. A user who has experienced using the system firsthand and has fully internalized how it can be used will be much better equipped to trust and use the system once it has gone live.

Our research shows that the key to training is variety. Holding face-to-face sessions in a classroom is a valuable tool for addressing questions and doubts, reflecting and discovering how others work with new technology, and considering the trickier aspects of a new system. Still, face-to-face sessions cannot be the only tool in the training toolbox, and the opportunity of meeting users face to face should not be squandered on lectures.

The most valuable training is where we train users to help themselves. Thus, any training program should be codesigned with users and should include self-training in sandboxes, eLearning, informal support, and training from frontline managers.

Users want to learn how to solve tricky problems in the future, not just operate simple tasks in a new system.

Give trainees the time to learn about the new systems and processes and to gain practical experience in a sandbox simulation environment. They must have time and support to absorb what they have learned. The earlier they are allowed to engage with the new systems and processes, the better prepared they will be.

The most surprising insight we discovered in our research was the power of training to generate feedback. Now we think of training as testing by different means. Like communication, though, we need to design a feedback loop into training. To do this, often we need to train, retrain, and retrain again.

Lever #7: Establishing Trust-Based Relationships

Everyone will agree that we are not just delivering technology within a set budget by an agreed-on deadline. The journey of the transformation matters as much as the outputs it creates. The journey and outputs combined result in the outcomes, benefits, and legacy we leave behind. Transformation projects provide a professional service – enabling this journey – and the key to all professional services is to be a trusted partner.

A transformation project asks internal and external experts to deliver change and technology by a deadline. The project must be trusted and the team working on it must be trusted advisors to the organization for the transformation's duration; this includes building trusted relationships with top-level managers and senior stakeholders as well as building trust-based relationships with end users.

Projects that create trust in the transformation and its solution are far more likely to succeed than projects that are either not trusted or are distrusted. While building trust requires time and effort, it is a worthwhile investment; when a project is trusted, the established relationship makes creating change much easier, because trust enables fast feedback, access to resources, and benefits realization. .

While trust *is* built through credibility and reliability, credibility and reliability are not the complete story. Typically, leaders sell their transformation by saying: "We have done it before" (credibility) and "We will do it again" (reliability). The complete "equation" also requires building intimacy and avoiding self-orientation. Even if strangers are fully qualified, they offer end users no real reason to trust them – there is no relationship.

We frequently notice in our research, however, that trust-building efforts can be one-sided. As transformation leaders, we find it easier to focus on building trust with stakeholders, sponsors, and key decision makers while spending less time or effort on end users.

Trust from stakeholders and sponsors sustains the transformation effort, but it is the end users who are vital to its ultimate success. If your end users don't trust the solution or new processes the transformation implements, they have no reason to use it.

Different actions are needed to build trust-based relationships with stakeholders and end users. For stakeholders, orientation toward a shared goal (a clear you win, I win) and creating intimacy through psychological safety are critical. For end users, credibility, in addition to the common goals and intimacy, is essential.

For this reason, it is clear that the organization's management – particularly frontline managers for end users – is an invaluable resource in building trust in the project. In our interviews, three out of four projects were initially viewed with suspicion.

In those projects, users' preexisting relationships with frontline managers were excellent ways to borrow trust. At the same time, the transformation develops its relationship with the user community. Make sure that end users understand the credibility of the project team and what is in it for them, and build a safe space to openly share pain points – achieve this, and they will trust the project and the change.

Put It into Practice

Our research found that not all seven levers are equally important. We found that, in order of importance, these four levers had a statistically significant link to success:

- Establishing trust-based relationships (Lever #7)
- Effective, dialogue-based communication (Lever #5)
- Effective training (Lever #6)
- Management ownership (Lever #4)

The other three levers – a clear reason for change (Lever #1), a defined approach to managing change (Lever #2), and early involvement of users (Lever #3) – were *not* statistically significantly linked to success; the value they offered indirectly contributed to success.

In managing technological and organizational change, don't assume that you need to implement all seven levers in your transformation simultaneously and perfectly. As each of the seven levers generally reinforces the others, by focusing on implementing the top four levers of change well, you will enjoy benefits from the others as a side effect.

Most important, consider your transformation. Where does it stand? Where can you make choices to increase your chances of success? Like us, you are the designer of your transformation's success.

Our Final Thoughts

Managing change often is challenging and abstract. Being responsible for helping an entire organization understand and embrace change is intimidating. The fact that there are countless frameworks and structures for managing change only complicates things.

When faced with such a challenge, it is easy to focus on what appear to be the more concrete and achievable tasks first. Often we start by polishing and refining the most brilliant reason for change or a perfectly defined strategy. It could be focusing your attention on ensuring the key sponsors are on board and owning the transformation. Or it could be the joy of putting out little fires every day.

These are all important tasks; however, devoting all your attention to them neglects the one factor that has the most impact on the transformation's success: building trust and confidence in the project.

As managing change is a variable and relative process requiring you to adapt to the situation at hand continually, you need to be in the field as much as possible. Time spent in the organization doing things and talking to end users, frontline managers, and middle managers is more valuable than time spent perfecting your strategy in the project room.

Appendix A – Coda – Change Management in Action

Throughout this book, we have referred to various organizations that have benefited from a structured approach to change management. Arla Foods is one such organization.

Arla Foods is a global dairy cooperative and one of the largest dairy companies in the world. With roots dating back to the 1880s, Arla Foods was officially formed in 2000 through a merger between two prominent Scandinavian dairy cooperatives. As a cooperative, Arla Foods follows a unique business model where its farmers have a direct ownership stake in the company.

Arla Foods is renowned for its wide range of dairy products, including milk, cheese, butter, cream, yogurt, and various specialty products. With a presence in over 100 countries, Arla Foods serves millions of consumers worldwide.

Overall, Arla Foods is a leading player in the global dairy industry. It combines the expertise of its cooperative farmers, a commitment to sustainability, and a dedication to delivering delicious and nutritious dairy products to consumers worldwide.

Implement Consulting Group has a long-standing relationship supporting Arla Foods' digital transformation. To get an insight into what change management looks like in action and how what we have described throughout this book plays out in real life, we have asked Marie Toftgaard, a change manager at Arla Foods, to talk us through her role and how she supports change projects for the company.

Change Management at Arla Foods – by Marie Toftgaard

At Arla Foods, our approach to change management is based on the Prosci framework, which includes ADKAR. In Arla IT, change management is part of the Agile Release Train (ART). My role in Arla Foods is as a business change manager within the planning ART.

(continued)

(continued)

I have three colleagues on the release train management team: the release train engineer, the release train architect, and the product manager. Together, we lead the train.

As I am the only one with this specific role in the train, I support new development tasks and am responsible for integrating change management with the development tasks.

Each release train within Arla IT can be very different. Therefore, my role in my specific train is not very operational – I don't do many of the change management plans myself, but I focus more on the conceptual side. Generally, when we are trying to move into new ways of working, I try it out and prototype it for the first time.

From there, I share with the teams what I have learned from the prototypes. As our understanding of the processes and requirements matures, I transfer ownership of these processes from myself to the teams, who will implement them from there.

Therefore, my focus often relates more to several of the seven levers in this book – I frequently find myself working with the product owners of the various teams on a range of essential tasks.

They may need to create a stakeholder map to understand which stakeholders and end users are involved in the change. Or, it might be an engagement plan, which provides a structured scheme for how the various stakeholders, managers, and end users are included in the project.

In addition, project leads might occasionally ask me to provide input and suggestions on training plans. Other tasks include stepping in for operational matters where other teams need more skills and managing or directing communication tasks.

One specific example involves creating videos together with the product owners. These stakeholder information and training videos were an exciting application of new technologies – they were made using AI.

Challenges in Change Management

I see the most significant challenge in change management as people forgetting that there is a "people side" of change – we're all so focused on the IT/tech side of change that we tend to underestimate the impact of change on the end users.

There might be an awareness that this people aspect exists, but sometimes those in charge of the project must learn the full benefit and potential of acknowledging and managing it.

It is common for stakeholders and those involved in development to become successful by specializing deeply in their specific field. As a result, change management and people are outside their comfort zone.

It is much easier for IT specialists and stakeholders to customize an SAP system – something they are experts in and have been promoted to their position for being specialists at – than to communicate about and build trust in that system. Since they don't have the same level of understanding and comfort with change management as they do with technical products, IT specialists and stakeholders are less comfortable talking about the change itself.

This means that when top management approaches stakeholders about a project, the stakeholders will focus on what they can do and feel they are experts at; they sometimes avoid having the negative conversation of "I am not an expert in this area and am not comfortable with it; however, I acknowledge it is still very important."

As a result, it is possible that top management needs to be made aware of how crucial managing organizational change is to a project. Thankfully, in my experience, this is changing – more and more, top management is becoming aware that change management actually is crucial.

This is not just happening at Arla either. That's why we reach out and consult with other organizations working on similar projects to our own. The first recommendation other projects give us is always: "Don't forget about change management."

The Cost of Failing at Change Management

In my experience, failing at change management carries a risk: The return on investment will not be as high as it could have been.

You might have the latest, state-of-the-art technology, but your end users need to use it how it is intended to be used. They might be unwilling to use it, or perhaps the training is inadequate – it might take longer than you anticipated for them to learn how to use the new technology effectively.

(continued)

(continued)

Solution

In the field, the level of skill and awareness regarding change management in general needs to be improved and overhauled. A development team needs to have the competencies within the team itself rather than these competencies being focused entirely on one person who holds the role of change manager.

While at least one person on the team should be an expert, more people must understand the concepts, terminology, and why managing change is essential. This means that instead of having the technical implementation and the people focus operating separately, the team can present a united front – being able to challenge and support each other – which ultimately empowers them to fill their roles even better.

What Is Arla Foods Working On?

We have been working on a major project for more than a year. As it is a huge change management task, we must sharpen our change management skills.

Currently, the people employed in the project are mainly IT specialists working on development. However, change management should start earlier. Generally speaking, many tech resources are engaged at the start, but their importance decreases throughout the project. In contrast, change management resources at work in the project generally start small and grow over time. I feel this should be the other way around – if not wholly, then at least a more balanced approach is needed.

Too often, it is discovered that change management is needed on a project only after development has started. At this point, the solution has already been decided on.

If change management specialists had been involved earlier, the solution might have been different. For instance, when providing end users with a new system, there might be something in the user interface that needs to be developed in a certain way. Bringing in change management early could help the solution become more intuitive and user-friendly than what might be decided on otherwise.

Change Management Accelerates Drawn-Out Projects

This is a powerful argument for applying change management far earlier in any project. I often see others notice these benefits once they have been introduced to the concepts and techniques behind change management.

They realized that end users are unmotivated and disengaged with training on new systems because the first part of the process – creating motivation and desire to support the change early on – has been overlooked. In such cases, the team would need to start again and begin communicating clearly to develop the desire and motivation of the end users to engage with the new systems and training.

If change management is applied from the start, the project is based on meeting both the organization's and the end users' needs. This helps the project run more efficiently and effectively. It also saves the need to invest additional resources later once you realize that end users are struggling to become emotionally invested or to buy in.

This emotional design and buy-in are important – it is easy to forget that it takes time to motivate people to adopt something new. People have their own struggles already, so we bring in something that we think they will value and expect them to welcome it automatically. The problem is that they are focused on their everyday challenges; with no reason to be interested in our new solution, they won't engage with it.

A specialist in the technical aspect of project design typically does not have the competencies to walk in somebody else's shoes, yet this is what this task requires. Change management specializes in understanding what would make someone who spends their day putting out fires excited to spend time and energy learning about a new tool and way of working.

Where Change Management Competencies Come From

The question then becomes: Where will this ability with change management in a company come from?

On one hand, it is crucial to create these competencies in existing employees – by upskilling specialists, for example. On the other hand, bringing in and hiring more change managers also is a viable solution.

In addition, more experienced or senior employees should be reminded of the importance of change management strategies. When a project lead understands that it is vital to translate the project's benefits to something more personal to the end users – such as what this would gain them for their personal development – the project is much more likely to succeed when rolled out.

(continued)

(continued)

The Future of Change Management

Change management will become more necessary in the future. Younger individuals coming into the company fresh from university might have different expectations about how they should be motivated to engage with things – they are more likely to say "You think we should do this? One way or another, convince me, or I won't do it."

Change management in the future will be a vital part of making change projects run more effectively and efficiently. Another example beyond helping the project get off the ground and driving end user acceptance and motivation is improving training.

Following the COVID-19 pandemic, we have learned to harness the power of online training – we don't need to rely on on-site classrooms as much as we used to. This area will improve rapidly in the future. Embodying the power of change management and effective training will help us deliver more personalized and customized training.

Doing this will allow us to target the information that the end user needs to know specifically and deliver it in the most effective way.

While it will be company-specific, embracing change management and investing in making it a part of all change projects from the start will be a game changer. Technology is innovating faster and faster; ensuring that the implementation of the new and innovative systems operates as smoothly and efficiently as possible will be vital.

Appendix B – Statistical Results in Detail

Description of the Data

We collected the data for this book by approaching organizations that recently completed a major technology transformation. We used our professional networks to approach potential informants in these organizations.

In total, we collected data from 155 projects, which were carried out by 117 different organizations. Of the projects, 66% were from the private sector, 32% from the public sector, and 2% from nonprofit organizations. The final investment decision for the projects was between 2003 and 2017, and they went live between 2007 and 2018.

These projects were initially planned to take between 2 and 72 months. The mean duration was 17 months, and the median duration was 14 months. The actual duration ranged from 2 to 60 months, with a mean duration of 20 months and a median duration of 17 months.

Factor Analysis of Success

Before building the regression model, we extracted factors for success, trust, and management ownership.

The factors of success comprised:

- Perceived success by the project sponsor, measured on a 10-point Likert scale
- Perceived success by end users, measured on a 10-point Likert scale
- Perceived success by front-line managers, measured on a 10-point Likert scale
- Perceived success by the project managers, measured on a 10-point Likert scale
- End user adoption of the system, measured on a 10-point Likert scale
- Achieving the impact intended, measured on a 10-point Likert scale
- Cost overrun, calculated as *ln(actual/estimated cost)*
- Schedule overrun, calculated as *ln(actual/estimated schedule)*
- Benefits overrun, calculated as *ln(actual/estimated benefits)*

The cost, schedule, and benefits estimates were retrieved from documents on the final investment decision, sometimes called the full or final business case. Actuals were taken from project accounts and postcompletion reports. These numbers came from documentary evidence about the projects.

The resulting factor solution suggested the extraction of two factors: one dimension mostly loaded by cost and schedule overrun, explaining 16% of the variation in the data, and a second dimension comprising all other factors, including benefits overrun, explaining 56% of the variation in the data.

We interpreted the first factor as *project management success* and the second factor as the *success of the transformation*.

The project management success factor represents the project's cost and schedule overruns. Transformation success represents the results and benefits measured we itemized above.

Factor Analysis of the Levers

First, we measured trust by the degree to which the project established trust-based relationships with (i) stakeholders and (ii) end users. Both factors used a 10-point Likert scale. The combined single factor explained 69% of the variation in the data.

Second, for management ownership, we extracted a single factor from nine variables, which was the degree to which top, middle, and frontline management supported, promoted, or owned the project. This factor was a three-by-three grid of these characteristics. Each characteristic was again measured on a 10-point Likert scale. The resulting variable extracted 49% of the variation in the data.

We considered an alternative factor solution that extracted a factor for each top, middle, and frontline management that comprised three variables: support, promotion, and ownership of the project. For these factors, the extracted variation was 84% (top management), 87% (middle management), and 88% (frontline management), respectively.

The other variables included in our model were:

- Clear reason for change, overall effectiveness of the training, and over-all effectiveness of the communication are all measured on a 10-point Likert scale.
- The time at which end users were first involved was measured by project progress in 10-percentage-point increments, that is, a 10-point scale, where 5 represented 50% complete or the project's midpoint.
- Whether the project had a defined approach to the change was measured as a binary yes/no question.

Regression Models

A multilevel and standard regression model was used to estimate the effects of each factor on the transformation and project management success – the two dimensions of our success factor. For the first analysis, we treated the organization as a random effect to account for differences between organizations. However, the random effect did not add any meaningful information to the model – the two models were identical in their estimates of the relative strengths of impact and their likelihood to be an effect.

The linear models were fitted using a Bayesian approach. We chose a Bayesian approach for this analysis because the first exploratory regression models using a conventional null-hypothesis significance-testing approach (NHST) returned nonsignificant findings. The Bayesian approach allows us to express confidence in finding no effect.

Unlike traditional NHST, Bayesian analysis yields complete distributional information regarding the parameters in the regression model.

The Bayesian analysis uses only the observed data and does not use p-values and confidence intervals based on hypothetical unobserved data. NHST assumes that the researcher stopped data collection because the predefined sample size was met – an assumption that does not apply to our data or to very few analyses.

Bayesian analyses are evaluated based on the posterior samples of a parameter, which are summarized with the credible interval (also called the highest density interval). In the case of linear regressions, we are interested in the credible intervals of the coefficient estimate of a parameter. If a parameter does not affect our criterion – that is, if the coefficient is zero – Bayesian analysis can accept the null value and not only reject it, as in NHST. For example, the conventional NHST using a regression model would find no statistically significant difference ($p = 0.754$). In NHST, all insignificant results have the same interpretation: $p = 0.075$ or $p = 0.75$.

We used Bayes factors to interpret the hypotheses in the model. A Bayes factor expresses the probability of a hypothesis. In a regression model, this can be interpreted as the probability that a variable in the regression model has an effect greater or smaller than zero – that is, no effect, given the data. For example, a Bayes factor of 100 means that, given the data, the hypothesis has a 100 times greater probability of being true than the opposite hypothesis.

To aid interpretation of the Bayes factors, we followed Jeffreys's interpretation of Bayes factors, as shown in Table B.1.

In our regression models, we used weakly informative priors. For regression coefficients, we set the prior at $N(0, 2)$ (i.e., a normal distribution with mean zero indicating no effect and standard deviation 2).

TABLE B.1 Bayes factors and their interpretation.

Bayes factor	Interpretation	Notation in our models
$1 < BF \leq 3$	Not statistically significant	
$3 < BF \leq 30$	Weak positive evidence	
$30 < BF \leq 100$	Statistically significant	*
>100	Highly statistically significant	**

Source: Adapted from Jeffreys (1961).

All models in this study were fitted using four chains and 10,000 draws after a warm-up of 1,000 draws. The resulting chains were well mixed. Auto-correlation in the chains was low. The divergence of chains was small. The posterior distributions were well balanced. However, in the multilevel model, the posterior for the organization-level effect could have been better balanced. It was not symmetrical and showed a fatter upper tail.

The problem with the multi-level model is most likely due to the small sample sizes of observations for some organizations (i.e., an effect due to an unbalanced sample). Thus, unsurprisingly, the simple model without a random effect performed better than the multi-level model.

All parameters had an effective sample size greater than 10% of the total sample. No parameters had a standard error greater than 10% of the posterior standard deviation. All Monte Carlo estimation errors were well below 10% of the posterior standard deviation.

The complete model results are shown in Table B.2.

The table shows the model that best describes the data concerning our identified transformation levers. Figure B.1 graphically depicts the estimated effect sizes and their uncertainty.

The figure illustrates the larger ranges of uncertainties of the nonsignificant factors, the structured approach to change, and the clear vision. It also shows that the nonsignificant finding about early user involvement has a comparatively small range of uncertainty in the estimated effect. This means our finding that early user involvement is not associated with transformation or project management success is robust.

The data show – at a high level of statistical significance – that trust and communication are key levers in relation to the transformation's success. In our data, the positive effect of increasing the transformation's success is more than 100 times more likely to be true than not (specifically, the Bayes factors are 8,999 and 181).

The next important lever is the effectiveness of training, which has a Bayes factor of 95 that is, it is 95 times more likely to have a positive effect

TABLE B.2 Result of fitting a Bayesian multiple regression model for transformation success and project management success to the data.

Response	Term	Estimate	Std. error	Conf. low	Conf. high	Bayes factor	
Transformation success	(Intercept)	−3.57	0.87	−5.27	−1.87	35999.00	**
	Trust	0.59	0.15	0.29	0.89	8999.00	**
	Management ownership	0.15	0.08	0.00	0.31	34.36	*
	Clear reason	0.12	0.13	−0.14	0.38	4.60	
	Communication	0.27	0.11	0.06	0.48	180.82	**
	Training	0.23	0.10	0.04	0.42	95.51	*
	Defined approach	0.55	0.33	−0.11	1.20	18.57	
	Early user involvement	−0.01	0.07	−0.14	0.13	1.16	
Project management success	(Intercept)	0.45	0.54	−0.59	1.51	4.02	
	Trust	−0.08	0.09	−0.27	0.10	4.51	
	Management ownership	0.04	0.05	−0.05	0.14	4.51	
	Clear reason	−0.01	0.08	−0.17	0.15	1.30	
	Communication	0.12	0.07	−0.01	0.25	29.00	
	Training	−0.13	0.06	−0.25	−0.01	61.28	*
	Defined approach	−0.62	0.21	−1.03	−0.22	630.58	**
	Early user involvement	0.03	0.04	−0.05	0.11	3.11	
Transformation success	sd(Observation)	1.72	0.11	1.52	1.96		
Project management success	sd(Observation)	1.06	0.07	0.94	1.21		

The columns report the mean estimate of the effect (coefficient) of the variable, the standard error of the mean estimate, the lower and higher bound of the 95% confidence interval (highest density interval), and the Bayes factor testing the hypothesis that the mean estimate of the effect differs from zero. Bayes factors above 30 are considered statistically significant (denoted *), and Bayes factors above 100 are considered highly statistically significant (denoted **).

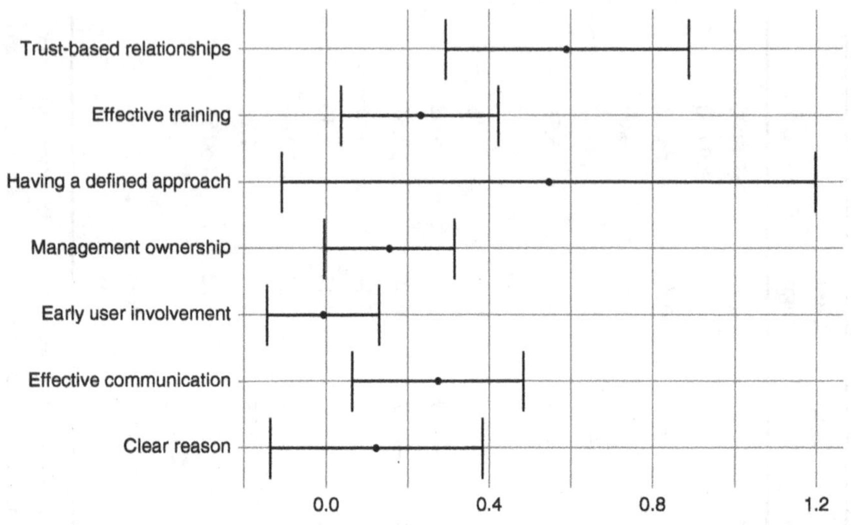

FIGURE B.1 Coefficient plot for the transformation success regression model fitted to the data. The mean estimate of the effect size of the coefficient (points) and the 95% Bayesian confidence interval (whiskers) are shown. The effect is not statistically significant, where zero is included in the confidence intervals.

on success than not – and management ownership, which is 34 times more likely to have a positive effect than not influencing success.

Notably, for the not statistically significant levers of clear reason and defined approach to change, we see a positive relation to the success of transformation. Yet the relationship is not strong enough to draw firm statistical conclusions. However, we find no support for the lever of early user involvement. Given our data, the effect of this lever is as likely to be associated with success as it is not.

Regarding project management success – that is, cost and schedule overruns – the only factors we identified with a statistically significant association are training effectiveness (BF = 61) and structured approach (BF = 630). Both factors reduce the likelihood of overspending and delays.

Lever #1: Clear Reason For Change

The regression model found no statistically significant relationship between clarity of reason and transformation success. The mean effect size is estimated at 0.12 with a confidence interval including zero (the HDI ranges from

−0.14 to 0.38) and a Bayes factor of only 4.6 for a positive effect. Thus, we concluded that a clear reason for change is not statistically significantly associated with the success of the transformation.

The regression fit for the association between the clear reason for change and project management success comes to the same conclusion. The factor is not statistically significant (the mean estimate of the effect is −0.01, HDI ranges from −0.17 to 0.15, and the Bayes factor for a negative effect is only 1.30).

To explain why this assumed factor is not associated with the success of the transformation, we iteratively built a model of other assumed characteristics, which we hypothesized to be related to a clear reason.

Those characteristics included the degree to which …

- the reason for the change was defined as a burning platform.
- the project had an appealing vision of the future you wanted to reach.
- the end users understood the reason for the change.
- the benefits of the project were defined.
- the project actively managed the benefits throughout the project life cycle.

In addition, we hypothesized that clear reason for change is needed to build a positive attitude toward the change. We also knew from our regression model that in the absence of a direct association between the success of the transformation and clear reason for change, an indirect effect, if any, would likely be with one of the statistically significant factors.

The correlation matrix of the factors indicated that clear reason for change has the strongest correlations with the effectiveness of communication and trust ($r = 0.36$ and $r = 0.22$, respectively).

Investigating a possible indirect effect on communication effectiveness, we found no statistically significant association of any of the variables we considered thematically close to clear reason for change. The only statistically significant association we found was the degree to which benefits were managed ($p = 0.003$, conventional null hypothesis testing in a regression model).

The analysis of clarity through vision through the associated characteristics was more fruitful and yielded a statistically significant model. The overall model fit was adequate: The comparative fit index (CFI) is 0.945, near the conventional cut-off at 0.95, and the Tucker–Lewis Index (TLI) is 0.914. The root mean square error of approximation (RMSEA) is 0.057, near the conventional cut-off at 0.05. The standardized root mean square residual (SRMR) is 0.053, below the traditional cut-off of 0.08.

Figure B.2 shows the final model of the variables associated with a clear reason for change. The notable insight here is that clarity of vision influences the degree to which benefits are defined. The greater the degree to which benefits are defined influences the trust of stakeholders. Stakeholder trust is directly and indirectly through end-user trust associated with the transformation's success.

The hypothesized pathway of clarity of vision to end-user trust was more complex. Here, the chain of influences found a positive effect between the clarity of vision and the degree to which benefits were defined. The degree to which benefits were defined and the degree to which the reason for the

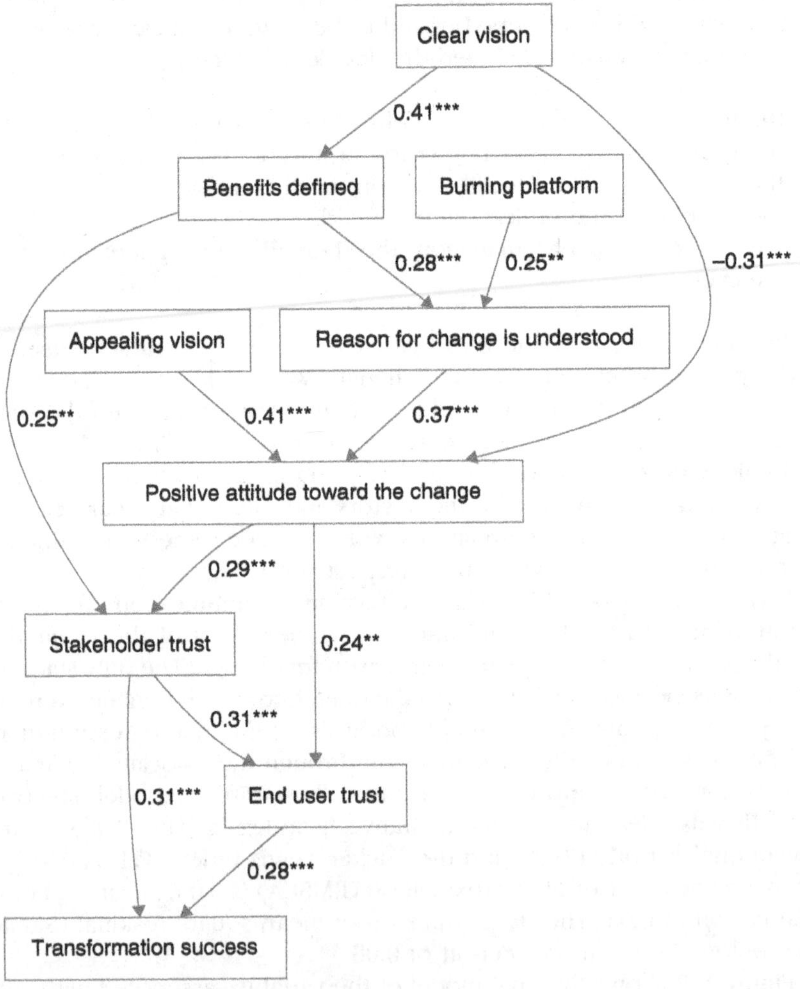

FIGURE B.2 Indirect effects of clear vision on transformation success. The figure shows only coefficients of statistically significant paths. Stars indicate statistical significance: *** $p \leq 0.001$, ** $p \leq 0.01$, * $p \leq 0.05$.

change was a burning platform has a statistically significant influence on the degree to which end users understand the reason for the change. Understanding the reason for the change and the degree to which the reason for the change was an appealing vision created a positive attitude toward the change, which in turn influences the levels of trust with end users and stakeholders and, ultimately, transformation success.

Notably, we also found a negative direct effect where the clarity of vision negatively influences the positive attitude toward the change. As described in Chapter 4, the follow-up questions in our interviews found that this has to do with the desire of end users and stakeholders to be part of a co-creation process of the vision. The clearer the vision for the change is defined at the outset, the greater the negative attitude toward the change – in effect, non-commitment, if not outright resistance.

Lever #2: Defined Approach to the Change

Whether the project had a defined approach to the change or not did not significantly influence the transformation success in the model fitted to our data. The mean estimate of the effect was 0.55, greater than the size of other effects. However, the defined approach to change was measured as a binary variable, which explains the effect size but lacks statistical significance (the 95% HDI includes zero, ranges from −0.11 to 1.20, and the Bayes factor of a positive effect is 18.57).

Conversely, a defined approach to change had a statistically significant negative effect on the project management success – that is, a defined approach is associated with lower cost and schedule overruns (mean estimate of the effect = −0.62, HDI ranges from −1.03 to 0.22 and does not include zero, Bayes factor of a negative effect is 630.58).

Figure B.3 shows the model of indirect effects that best fits the data. The overall model fit was barely adequate, with CFI = 0.985, TLI = 0.826, RMSEA = 0.084, and SRMR = 0.0907. The key reason is that other factors explain the transformation success much better and that in our survey design, we relied on three binary variables in this model, which have much lower variation in the data than Likert-scaled variables.

Yet the model shows a statistically significant pathway. Having a defined approach is likely to lead to having dedicated change resources. With dedicated change resources, a project is more likely to have a dedicated change budget. A dedicated change budget leads to a higher degree of the project following the defined approach to change, which ultimately is statistically significantly associated with transformation success.

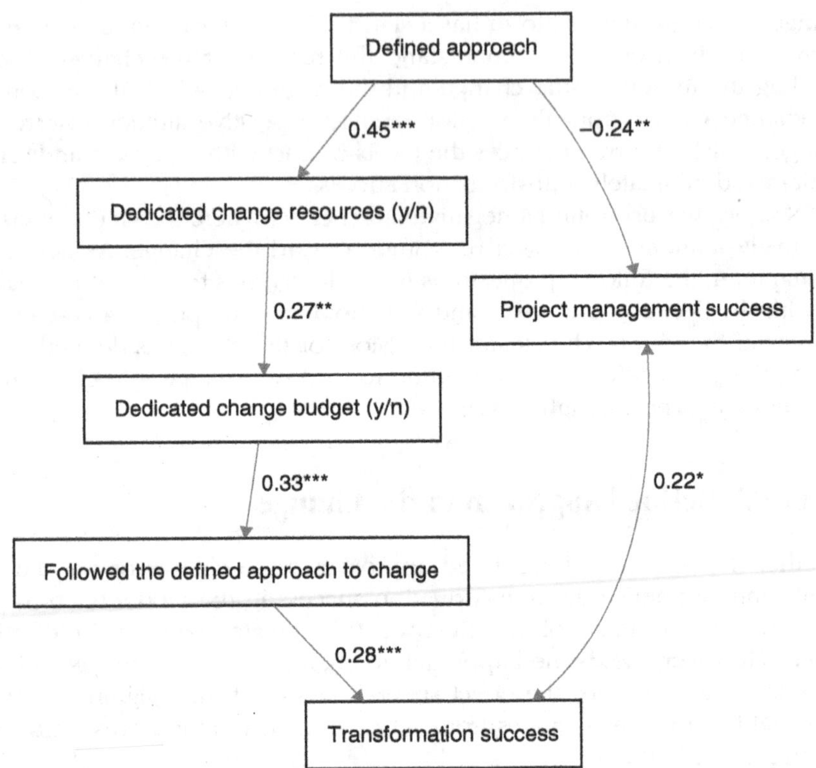

FIGURE B.3 Indirect effects of defined approach on project management and transformation success. (Note the effect size between defined approach and project management success differs from the regression model due to the inclusion of the statistically significant covariance between transformation and project management success.) The figure shows only coefficients of statistically significant paths. Stars indicate statistical significance: *** $p \leq 0.001$, ** $p \leq 0.01$, * $p \leq 0.05$.

Lever #3: Early User Involvement

Our model did not find a statistically significant effect of early user involvement with transformation success (effect estimate = −0.01, HDI from −0.14 to 0.13, Bayes factor 1.16) or project management success (effect estimate = 0.03, HDI from −0.05 to 0.11, Bayes factor 3.11).

We hypothesized initially that early user involvement might be associated with the activities that users get involved in. In particular, we asked in our interviews about users' involvement in systems design, process design, and testing.

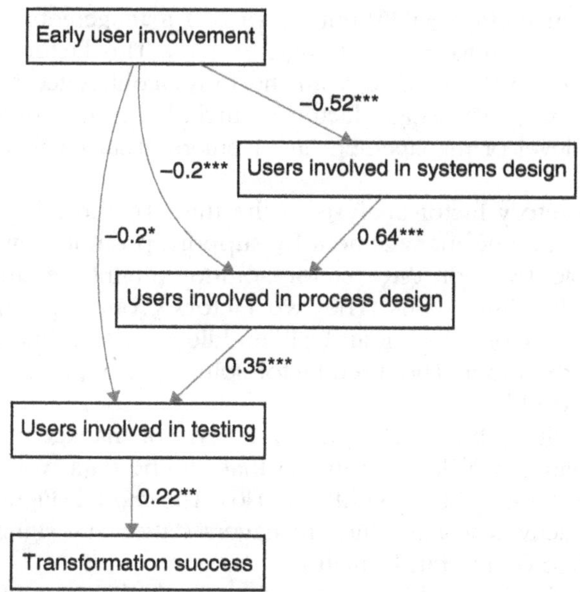

FIGURE B.4 Model of the indirect effects of early user involvement associated with transformation success. The figure shows only coefficients of statistically significant paths. Stars indicate statistical significance: *** $p \leq 0.001$, ** $p \leq 0.01$, * $p \leq 0.05$.

We used a structural equation modeling approach to model the indirect effects of early user involvement (Figure B.4). The final model is a very good fit for the data (CFI = 0.999, TFL = 0.997, RMSEA = 0.020, SRMR = 0.040).

For the model interpretation, it is crucial to understand that the variable early end user involvement was measured by approximating the point of completion when users were first involved (<10% complete, <20% complete, ..., <100% complete). The model shows that early user involvement is associated with involving users in the design of systems and processes and testing. What the model finds is, however, that neither the involvement in process or systems design nor early involvement overall has a direct effect on the success of the transformation. Only testing has a direct influence on success. The other activities support or enable user involvement in testing.

Lever #4: Management Ownership

Our model finds that management ownership has a direct link to the success of transformations (mean effect estimate = 0.15, HDI from 0.00 to 0.89, Bayes factor of a positive effect 34.36) but not project management success (effect 0.04, HDI from −0.05 to 0.14, Bayes factor 4.51). This factor is the weakest significant factor in the models, with the lower confidence interval bound being close to zero. The single factor we included in the regression model measures the level of management involvement at all levels and across all activities.

The exploratory factor analysis of the three-by-three grid of variables (top, middle, frontline management by support, promote, own) suggested that a possible two- or three-factor solution might be an appropriate reduction of the dimensions. The two factors group all activities of top management into one factor and all middle and frontline management activities into the other. The three-factor solution groups activities by each management level.[1]

If we introduce three factors for each level of management combining the three activities, we derive a model that fits the data well (CFI = 0.974, TLI = 0.961, RMSEA = 0.079, SRMR = 0.040). The model (Figure B.5) shows that only the activities of frontline managers statistically significantly influence the success of the transformation.

However, if we take this factor on its own and disregard the activities of middle and top management, the overall regression model, including the other six levers of change, finds that frontline management involvement alone does not statistically significantly influence success above and beyond the other six levers.

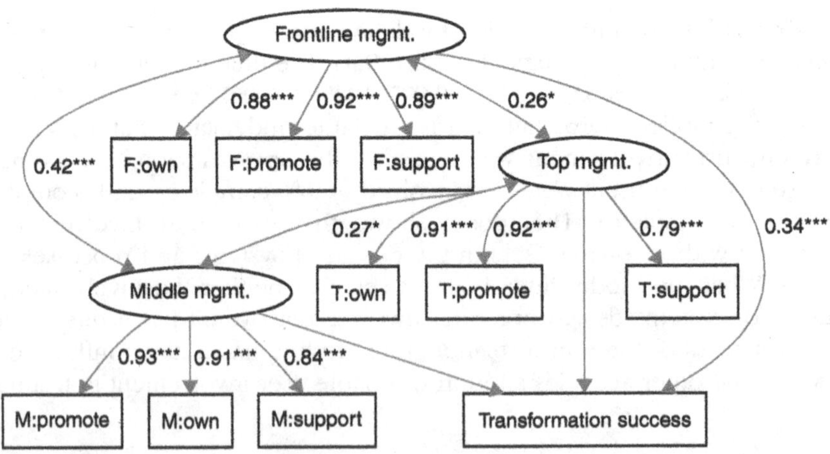

FIGURE B.5 Full model of management ownership and transformation success (F = Frontline management, M = Middle management, F = frontline management). The figure shows only coefficients of statistically significant paths. Stars indicate statistical significance: *** p ≤ 0.001, ** p ≤ 0.01, * p ≤ 0.05.

Lever #5: Effective Communication

The degree of communication effectiveness has a statistically significant influence on the success of the transformation (mean effect estimate = 0.27, HDI from 0.06 to 0.48, Bayes factor 180.82) but not project management success (effect = 0.12, HDI from −0.01 to 0.25, Bayes factor 29.00).

Modeling our hypothesized factors influencing communication effectiveness yields a good fit model (CFI = 1.0, TLI = 1.0, RMSEA <0.001, SRMR = 0.034). In the final, parsimonious model (Figure B.6), the nonsignificant variables excluded are whether the project had a communications plan and how well the project supported frontline management.

Furthermore, in the model, we discovered that positive reinforcement as the focus of communication does not directly influence its effectiveness. However, the more communication is focused on positive reinforcement, the greater the level of dialogue and targeting, which increases communication effectiveness. The best model includes an indirect effect between the level of dialogue and the level to which the communication was targeted.

Next, we were interested in the content and effectiveness of the communication. Our data found no significant differences, whether the communication included the change, the new processes, new roles, project status, or the system. The only statistically significant difference we found was whether the communication included the benefits of the change (t-test p = 0.0366).

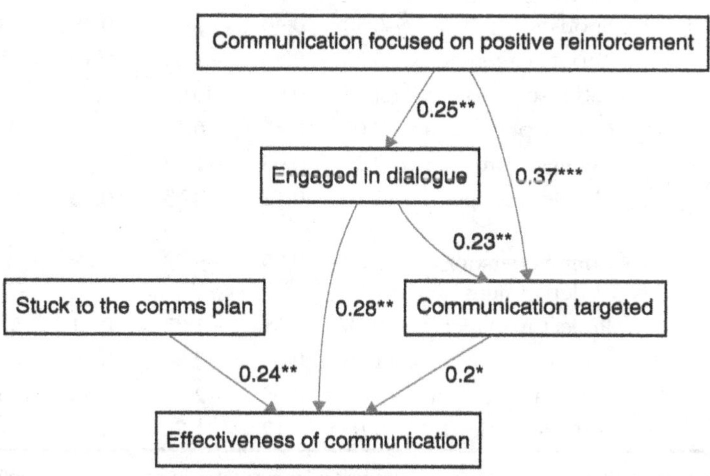

FIGURE B.6 Model for communication effectiveness. The figure shows only coefficients of statistically significant paths. Stars indicate statistical significance: *** p ≤ 0.001, ** p ≤ 0.01, * p ≤ 0.05.

TABLE B.3 Result of fitting a Bayesian multiple regression model for the effectiveness of communication and the degrees to which trust was built with stakeholders and end users depending on the key communicator of the change.

Dependent variable	Term	Estimate	Std. error	Conf. low	Conf. high	Bayes factor	
Communication effectiveness	(Intercept)	6.65	0.45	5.78	7.54	Inf	**
	Change team	0.03	0.60	−1.13	1.21	1.09	
	Middle management	−0.07	0.70	−1.44	1.32	1.16	
	Comms person/ department	0.76	0.95	−1.10	2.62	3.72	
	Project manager	−0.19	0.53	−1.24	0.84	1.8	
	Sponsor	−0.15	0.80	−1.74	1.42	1.34	
	Top management	0.11	0.61	−1.08	1.30	1.35	
	sd(Observation)	1.86	0.12	1.64	2.11		
Stakeholder trust	(Intercept)	0.36	0.27	−0.18	0.89	8.97	
	Change team	0.01	0.37	−0.72	0.72	1.02	
	Middle management	−0.15	0.42	−0.97	0.67	1.79	
	Comms person/ department	−1.22	0.54	−2.28	−0.16	78.82	**
	Project manager	−0.32	0.32	−0.95	0.31	5.31	
	Sponsor	−0.50	0.48	−1.46	0.45	5.66	
	Top management	−0.63	0.37	−1.35	0.10	21	
	sd(Observation)	1.13	0.07	1.00	1.28		
End user trust	(Intercept)	7.07	0.47	6.13	8.00	Inf	**
	Change team	−0.29	0.63	−1.52	0.94	2.13	
	Middle management	−1.30	0.72	−2.73	0.12	26.91	
	Comms person/ department	−1.87	0.99	−3.82	0.09	31.64	*
	Project manager	−0.59	0.55	−1.67	0.51	5.96	
	Sponsor	−1.20	0.84	−2.86	0.45	12.09	
	Top management	−1.56	0.65	−2.83	−0.30	133.33	**
	sd(Observation)	1.95	0.12	1.73	2.21		

The columns report the mean estimate of the key communicator in relation to the intercept, which is used as a reference level for the business unit/frontline management as the key communicator. The standard error of the mean estimate, the lower and higher bound of the 95% confidence interval (highest density interval), and the Bayes factor testing the hypothesis that the mean estimate of the effect differs from zero. Bayes factors above 30 are statistically significant (denoted *), and Bayes factors above 100 are highly statistically significant (denoted **).

Finally, we were interested in the effect of the key communicator. We asked the project who the key communicator was: top management, the project sponsor, the person or department responsible for communication, the project manager, middle management, the change team, or frontline management.

We considered three dependent variables: the effectiveness of the communication, the degree to which stakeholder trust was built, and the degree to which end user trust was built. Table B.3 shows the model's results with the reference level of frontline management. The comparison of the effectiveness of the communication shows no differences.

The model shows that the person or department responsible for communication built less trust (BF = 78.82) with stakeholders. For end user trust, the model shows that the communications person or department and top management built less trust when they were the key communicators (BF = 31.64 and BF = 133.33, respectively).

Lever #6: Effective Training

In our regression model, training was a statistically significant factor for both the transformation success (mean estimated effect = 0.23, HDI from 0.04 to 0.42, Bayes factor 95.51) and project management success (effect = −0.13, HDI from −0.25 to −0.01, Bayes factor 61.28).

We hypothesized that specific characteristics of the training might influence the effectiveness of training:

- Planning the training together with end users
- Designing the training together with end users
- Conducting the training together with end users
- Training includes future capabilities
- Early start of the training
- Late finish of the training
- Duration of training activities

However, in the model to investigate training effectiveness, we did not find any statistically significant influences on the start, end, or duration of training. Furthermore, we found no statistically significant influence on the degree to which future capabilities were included in the training. We also did not find any statistically significant effect on conducting training together with end users.

The model fits the data well (CFI = 1, TFL = 1, RMSEA<0.001, SRMR = 0.046). The model (Figure B.7) shows that planning the training with end users (coplanning) statistically significantly increases the level of designing the training together with end users (codesign). Codesign increases the effectiveness of training and the degree to which frontline managers prepare end users – the latter being a proxy for formal and informal training. The effectiveness of training and frontline managers' preparation of end users ultimately influence transformation success.

We hypothesized that the content of training might influence the effectiveness of the training or the degree to which frontline managers prepared end users for the change. The particular aspects of content we assumed to be relevant were:

- New capabilities required
- New competencies required
- New roles
- The new system
- New processes
- Changes in mindset

However, a model fitted to the data finds no statistically significant influence of any content on the effectiveness of training or the preparation of users by their frontline managers. The most likely interpretation is that the training content needs to be tailored for each transformation. Thus, no generalizable conclusions can be found across different transformations.

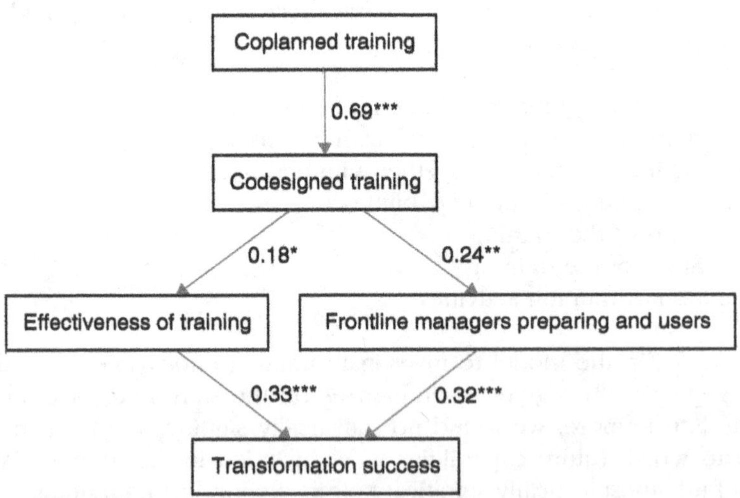

FIGURE B.7 Explanatory variables of training effectiveness and the relation to transformation success. The figure shows only coefficients of statistically significant paths. Stars indicate statistical significance: *** $p \leq 0.001$, ** $p \leq 0.01$, * $p \leq 0.05$.

Finally, we hypothesized that different channels for training have a different effect on the influence of training and the degree to which frontline managers prepared the end users for the change. The channels we investigated were:

- Classroom-based training
- One-to-one training
- eLearning
- Quick guides
- Webinars
- Self-guided training in a sandbox

In our analysis, we did not find any statistically significant differences between the training channels and their effectiveness. However, we found a statistically significant difference between the level of frontline managers preparing end users for the change and one channel: self-training in a sandbox or similar environment (mean estimated effect 1.73, HDI from 0.99 to 2.47, Bayes factor is infinite).

Lever #7: Establishing Trust-Based Relationships

The regression model we used to fit the seven levers to the data indicated that trust-based relationships with end users and stakeholders are the most critical lever for transformation success (mean estimate of the effect = 0.59, HDI ranges from 0.29 to 0.89, Bayes factor 8,999.00). On the other hand, the impact on project management success is not statistically significant (effect = −0.08, HDI from −0.27 to 0.10, Bayes factor 4.51).

We hypothesized Maister's trust formula when investigating the factors influencing the establishment of trust-based relationships. We adapted the formula to investigate the underlying ideas of the model that trust is the result of:

- Perceptions of having the needed competencies or experiences (credibility; i.e., trust built by words)
- Perceptions of delivering as promises (reliability; i.e., trust built by actions)
- The attitude toward the project (intimacy; i.e., trust built by emotions)
- Organizational goal orientation – that is, win-win focus (inverse of self-orientation; i.e., trust built by aligned motives)

The model fitted to the data (Figure B.8) shows that stakeholder trust is statistically significantly associated with the orientation toward joint goals

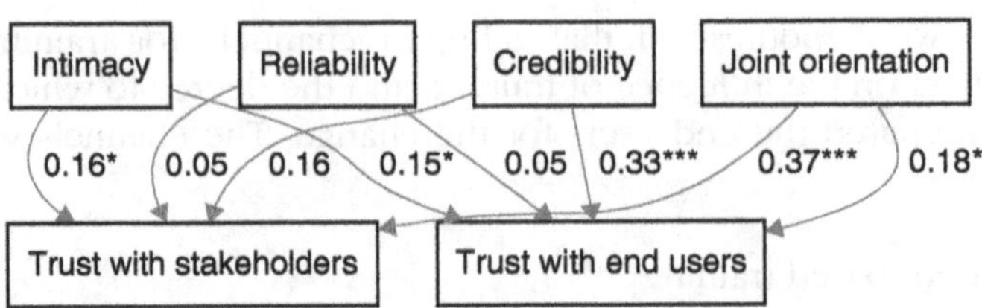

FIGURE B.8 Model of the trust equation factors associated with the trust-based relationships with stakeholders and end users. The figure shows all coefficients on the paths. Stars indicate statistical significance: *** $p \leq 0.001$, ** $p \leq 0.01$, * $p \leq 0.05$.

(effect 0.37, $p < 0.001$) and intimacy (effect 0.16, $p = 0.027$). In other words, we find that trust is most effectively built by aligning the motives of the project and the stakeholders. The second most effective way to build trust is through establishing intimacy (i.e., creating an emotionally and psychologically safe relationship where open and honest conversations and sharing can occur).

Trust with end users is statistically significantly associated with credibility (effect 0.33, $p < 0.001$), intimacy (effect 0.15, $p = 0.046$), and joint goals (effect 0.18, $p = 0.038$). The dimensions of building trust with end users are similar to the results from the analysis of stakeholder trust, with the addition that credibility is the most effective approach to building trust.

Testing the Influence of Complexity Factors

Finally, we conducted two robustness checks of the models. As part of our data collection, we also included questions that evaluate project complexity. From this perspective, complexity is the difficulty level of project delivery. The specific characteristics that make project delivery more difficult were derived from general work on projects,[2] approaches to software development estimation,[3] and the sociopolitical study of forecasting.[4]

The complexity factors from the project management field we included were:

- The goals, business case, and success criteria were clear.
- The project involved innovative technology.
- There were a large number of unknowns in the solution design.
- The project followed an incremental approach.
- The project deliverables were highly interdependent.
- The scope was minimal and stable.
- The project had an effective governance structure.

TABLE B.4 Result of fitting a Bayesian multiple regression model for transformation success and project management success to the data.

Response	Term	Estimate	Std. error	Conf. low	Conf. high	Bayes factor	
Transformation success	(Intercept)	−6.29	1.42	−9.10	−3.48	Inf	**
	Clear business case and goals	0.18	0.11	−0.03	0.41	19.50	
	Innovative technology	−0.04	0.08	−0.20	0.11	2.25	
	Unknowns in solution design	−0.09	0.09	−0.27	0.09	5.09	
	Incremental approach	0.01	0.07	−0.13	0.14	1.16	
	Interdepend deliverables	−0.07	0.09	−0.24	0.11	3.73	
	Minimal and stable scope	0.11	0.10	−0.10	0.31	5.86	
	Effective governance	0.42	0.10	0.22	0.62	35 999.00	**
	Shifting, competing requirements	0.12	0.10	−0.08	0.31	7.83	
	Influence over environment	0.09	0.09	−0.10	0.27	4.45	
	Uniqueness	−0.03	0.07	−0.17	0.11	1.97	
	Complex processing required	−0.07	0.10	−0.26	0.11	3.65	
	Reusability required	0.03	0.06	−0.09	0.16	2.39	
	High performance required	−0.10	0.08	−0.27	0.06	7.71	
	High security required	0.25	0.07	0.10	0.40	2570.00	**
	Political bias	0.02	0.07	−0.12	0.16	1.50	
	Track record used for comparison	0.02	0.06	−0.10	0.15	1.70	

(CONTINUED)

TABLE B.4 (CONTINUED)

Response	Term	Estimate	Std. error	Conf. low	Conf. high	Bayes factor
Project management success	(Intercept)	−1.26	0.78	−2.79	0.28	17.17
	Clear business case and goals	0.00	0.06	−0.12	0.12	1.10
	Innovative technology	0.05	0.04	−0.03	0.14	8.45
	Unknowns in solution design	0.09	0.05	−0.01	0.19	23.71
	Incremental approach	−0.05	0.04	−0.12	0.03	8.36
	Interdepend deliverables	0.02	0.05	−0.08	0.11	1.80
	Minimal and stable scope	−0.02	0.06	−0.13	0.10	1.63
	Effective governance	0.04	0.05	−0.07	0.14	2.96
	Shifting, competing requirements	0.05	0.05	−0.06	0.15	4.26
	Influence over environment	0.00	0.05	−0.10	0.10	1.01
	Uniqueness	−0.01	0.04	−0.08	0.07	1.50
	Complex processing required	−0.04	0.05	−0.15	0.06	4.08
	Reusability required	0.01	0.03	−0.06	0.08	1.56
	High performance required	0.07	0.05	−0.02	0.16	15.33
	High security required	0.01	0.04	−0.07	0.09	1.66
	Political bias	−0.01	0.04	−0.09	0.07	1.62
	Track record used for comparison	−0.03	0.04	−0.10	0.04	3.89
Transformation success	sd(Observation)	2.06	0.13	1.82	2.33	
Project management success	sd(Observation)	1.13	0.07	1.00	1.28	

The columns report the mean estimate of the effect (coefficient) of the variable, the standard error of the mean estimate, the lower and higher bound of the 95% confidence interval (highest density interval), and the Bayes factor testing the hypothesis that the mean estimate of the effect differs from zero. Bayes factors above 30 are considered statistically significant (denoted *), and Bayes factors above 100 are considered highly statistically significant (denoted **).

- The project had competing and shifting requirements.
- The project could influence its environment to achieve success.

The complexity factors from the software development field included were:

- The solution requires complex internal processing in the system.
- The solution needs to be reusable.
- The solution needs to fulfill high-performance requirements.
- Security aspects are very important for the solution.

The complexity factors from the sociopolitical study of forecasting were:

- This project is unique, so it is difficult to compare with other projects.
- The initial plan and business case showed political intent instead of the most likely outcome.
- The organizational unit has a historical record of past projects to which this business case was compared.

The results were fitted as with the above analysis using a Bayesian regression approach (Table B.4). Surprisingly, only two factors have a statistically significant association with transformation success. These are effective governance, which indicates lower complexity and, therefore, greater ease in delivering the transformation, and high-security requirements, which is unsurprising as a complexity factor. The finding that less complex governance influences the transformation success supports our main analysis, which shows the importance of trust-based relationships with stakeholders as discussed in Chapter 10. However, the analysis points to an impact opposite the one we hypothesized.

In the analysis, we found that higher security requirements led to greater transformation success, which is contrary to our expectations and those of the literature. This might be because cybersecurity is widely understood to be as much an organizational change as a technology change challenge.

None of the complexity factors had a statistically significant association with the project management success of the transformation.

Testing the Classic Project Management Success Factors

Finally, our second robustness check focussed on project management success factors. Our survey included a list of 11 commonly accepted success factors adapted from the meta-analysis of projects.[5] These factors included:

- Effectively monitored and controlled, e.g., by a PMO?
- Lead by a competent project manager(s)?

TABLE B.5 Result of fitting a Bayesian multiple regression model for transformation success and project management success to the data.

Response	Term	Estimate	Std. error	Conf. low	Conf. high	Bayes factor	
Transformation success	(Intercept)	−8.01	1.22	−10.42	−5.61	Inf	**
	Effective monitor and control	−0.02	0.09	−0.20	0.15	1.51	
	Competent project manager(s)	0.18	0.11	−0.03	0.39	19.33	
	Qualified and motivated team	0.15	0.13	−0.11	0.40	6.70	
	Detailed, up-to-date plan	0.03	0.11	−0.18	0.24	1.66	
	Realistic and reliable schedule	−0.01	0.08	−0.17	0.15	1.18	
	Lacking suitable staff	0.03	0.08	−0.13	0.20	1.93	
	Well-performing suppliers	0.09	0.08	−0.07	0.26	6.74	
	Robust contracts	0.06	0.09	−0.12	0.24	2.89	
	Sustainable mix of resources	0.01	0.08	−0.16	0.17	1.18	
	Effective risk management	0.26	0.09	0.08	0.44	345.15	**
	Stakeholder alignment	0.34	0.10	0.15	0.53	7199.00	**
Project management success	(Intercept)	−0.37	0.73	−1.81	1.08	2.24	
	Effective monitor and control	0.01	0.05	−0.10	0.11	1.17	
	Competent project manager(s)	0.02	0.07	−0.11	0.15	1.54	
	Qualified and motivated team	0.01	0.08	−0.14	0.17	1.29	
	Detailed, up-to-date plan	−0.02	0.06	−0.14	0.11	1.61	
	Realistic and reliable schedule	0.01	0.05	−0.08	0.11	1.51	
	Lacking suitable staff	0.01	0.05	−0.09	0.11	1.49	
	Well-performing suppliers	−0.09	0.05	−0.19	0.00	33.92	*
	Robust contracts	0.03	0.05	−0.07	0.14	2.74	
	Sustainable mix of resources	0.01	0.05	−0.09	0.11	1.32	
	Effective risk management	0.02	0.06	−0.09	0.13	1.70	
	Stakeholder alignment	0.04	0.06	−0.07	0.16	3.26	
Transformation success	sd(Observation)	1.93	0.12	1.71	2.19		
Project management success	sd(Observation)	1.16	0.07	1.03	1.32		

The columns report the mean estimate of the effect (coefficient) of the variable, the standard error of the mean estimate, the lower and higher bound of the 95% confidence interval (highest density interval), and the Bayes factor testing the hypothesis that the mean estimate of the effect differs from zero. Bayes factors above 30 are considered statistically significant (denoted *), and Bayes factors above 100 are considered highly statistically significant (denoted **).

- Carried out by a qualified and motivated team?
- Planned in detail and was the plan updated regularly?
- Following a realistic and reliable schedule?
- Lacking suitable staff?
- Good in communication among team members?
- Supported by well-performing suppliers?
- Employing robust supplier contracts with clear responsibilities?
- Using a sustainable mix of internal & external resources?
- Addressing and managing risks effectively?
- Able to align the major stakeholders?

As before, we fitted a Bayesian regression model to the data (Table B.5). The analysis finds that effective risk management and stakeholder alignment are associated with transformation success, and supplier performance is associated with project management success. We concluded that these findings support the main analysis. As discussed change management is not linear and therefore good risk management - the anticipation and management of uncertainties that might impact the transformation's objectives - is crucial. The finding that stakeholder alignment is essential supports the finding in the main analysis about the need to establish trust-based relationships with stakeholders, which is discussed in Chapter 10.

Notes

Introduction

1. Statistics and conclusions from this project can be found at http://www.healthpayrollinquiry.qld.gov.au.
2. Hornstein, H.A. (2015). The integration of project management and organizational change management is now a necessity. *International Journal of Project Management* 33 (2): 291–298.
3. Flyvbjerg, B. and Budzier, A. (2011). Why your IT project might be riskier than you think. *Harvard Business Review 89* (9).
   Flyvbjerg, B., Budzier, A., Lee, J.S. et al. (2022). The empirical reality of IT project cost overruns: discovering a power-law distribution. *Journal of Management Information Systems* 39 (3): 607–639.
4. This definition is adapted from Matt, C., Hess, T., and Benlian, A. (2015). Digital transformation strategies. *Business & Information Systems Engineering* 57: 339–343.
5. Adapted from Henriette, E., Feki, M., and Boughzala, I. (2015). The Shape of Digital Transformation: A Systematic Literature Review. *MCIS 2015 Proceedings*. 10. http://aisel.aisnet.org/mcis2015/10. Information Systems in a Changing Economy and Society, 431.

Chapter 1

1. March, J.G. (1991). Exploration and exploitation in organizational learning. *Organization Science* 2 (1): 71–87.
2. Farjoun, M. (2010). Beyond dualism: stability and change as a duality. *Academy of Management Review* 35 (2): 202–225.
3. Ibid.
4. Moran, J.W. and Brightman, B.K. (2001). Leading organizational change. *Career Development International* 9 (2): 111–118. https://doi.org/10.1108/13620430110383438.

5. Knowles, H.P. and Saxberg, B.O. (1988). Organizational leadership of planned and unplanned change: a systems approach to organizational viability. *Futures*, 20 (3), 252–265.

6. Ibid.

7. Flyvbjerg, B., Budzier, A., Lee, J.S. et al. (2022). The empirical reality of IT project cost overruns: Discovering a power-law distribution. *Journal of Management Information Systems* 39 (3): 607–639.

8. Knowles and Saxberg, 1988. Organizational leadership of planned and unplanned change.

9. Porras, J.I. and Silvers, R. (1991). Organization development and transformation. *Annual Review of Psychology* 42: 51–78.

10. Weick, K.E. and Quinn, R.E. (1999). Organizational change and development. *Annual Review of Psychology* 50 (1): 361–386.

11. Weick, K.E., Sutcliffe, K.M., and Obstfeld, D. (1999). Organizing for high reliability: Processes of high reliability. *Research in Organizational Behavior* 21: 81–123.

12. McNish, J. and Silcoff, S. (2015). *Losing the Signal: The Untold Story Behind the Extraordinary Rise and Spectacular Fall of BlackBerry.* Flatiron Books.

13. Whittle, A., Mueller, F., and Mangan, A. (2009). Storytelling and character: victims, villains and heroes in a case of technological change. *Organization* 16 (3): 425–442.

14. Goh, J.M. and Arenas, A.E. (2020). IT value creation in public sector: how IT-enabled capabilities mitigate tradeoffs in public organisations. *European Journal of Information Systems* 29 (1): 25–43.

15. Smith, E.D. and Nyman, R.C. (1939). *Technology & Labor: A Study of the Human Problems of Labor Saving*. Institute of Human Relations.

16. Ibid., 74.

17. Kotter, J.P. (1995). Leading change: Why transformation efforts fail. *Harvard Business Review*, May–June. https://hbr.org/1995/05/leading-change-why-transformation-efforts-fail-2&sa=D&source=docs&ust=1666601835036961&usg=AOvVaw1KIGcy7jgPaRnirWZLwdTz

18. Beck, K., Beedle, M., Van Bennekum, A., et al. (2001). Manifesto for agile software development. agilealliance.org.

19. Dreyfus, S.E. and Dreyfus, H.L. (1980). *A Five-Stage Model of the Mental Activities Involved in Directed Skill Acquisition*. Operations Research Center, University of California.
    Dreyfus, S.E. and Dreyfus, H.L. (1986). *Mind Over Machine*. Free Press.

20. Gigerenzer, G. and Gaissmaier, W. (2011). Heuristic decision making. *Annual Review of Psychology* 62 (1): 451–482.

21. Flyvbjerg, B. and Budzier, A. (2018). Ten Heuristics that Make Leaders of Projects and Programs Successful. Oxford Global Projects. Available at SSRN: https://ssrn.com/abstract=3226505

Chapter 2

1. DeLone, W. and McLean, E.R. (1992). Information systems success: The quest for the dependent variable. *Information Systems Research* 3 (1): 60–95.
2. For a structured review of developments in understanding success, see Jeyaraj, A. (2022). Models of information technology use: meta-review and research directions, *Journal of Computer Information Systems*. https://doi.org/10.1080/08874417.2022.2106462
3. Raskino, M., Moyer, K., Smith, S., and Vogel, G. (May 8, 2024). *2024 CEO Survey—The Year of Strategy Relaunches*. Gartner.
4. Schmidt, E. and Rosenberg, J. (2014). *How Google Works*. Grand Central Publishing.
5. Brynjolfsson, E. and Yang, S. (1996). Information technology and productivity: a review of the literature. *Advances in Computers* 43: 179–214.
6. Holweg, M., Staats, B.R., and Upton, D.M. (August 28, 2018). *Making process improvements stick* Kenan Institute of Private Enterprise Research Paper No. 18-22. Available at SSRN: https://ssrn.com/abstract=3240097 or http://dx.doi.org/10.2139/ssrn.3240097
7. Kotter, J.P. and Schlesinger, L.A. (1989). Choosing strategies for change. *Readings in Strategic Management* 1: 294–306.
8. Atkinson, R. (1999). Project management: cost, time and quality, two best guesses and a phenomenon, its [sic] time to accept other success criteria. *International Journal of Project Management* 17 (6): 337–342.
9. Sommer, M. and Svaneborg, T.G. (May 15, 2022). Medarbejdere flygter fra omstridt styrelse: *Der er så eklatant mangel på ordentlig ledelse, at folk løber skrigende væk* [Employees flee from controversial agency: "There is such a glaring lack of proper management that people run away screaming]. Børsen press release. https://borsen.dk/nyheder/virksomheder/medarbejdere-flygter-fra-omstridt-ejendomsstyrelse
10. See Appendix B for the factorial analysis.
11. Maylor, H., Geraldi, J., Budzier, A., Turner, N., and Johnson, M. (2023). Mind the gap: towards performance measurement beyond a plan-execute logic, *International Journal of Project Management*, 41(10).
12. Hubbard, D. W. 2014. *How to Measure Anything: Finding the Value of Intangibles in Business*. John Wiley.

13. We did not add here the wrongly attributed quote "If you can't measure it, you can't manage it," a quote that Peter Drucker never said and according to his own colleagues would most likely have disagreed with. See: https://www.drucker.institute/thedx/measurement-myopia
14. Hubbard, How to Measure Anything.
15. Sauer, C. (1993). *Why Information Systems Fail: A Case Study Approach*. Alfred Waller.

Chapter 3

1. At least at the outset. The famous example is the digital transformation of the Health Care Records System of the US Department of Veterans Affairs. This project started after the Vietnam War and, as of 2024, is still not finished. The project is as old as Intel and CompuServe.

Chapter 4

1. Budzier, A. and Flyvbjerg, B. (2011). Why your IT project might be riskier than you think. *Harvard Business Review* 89 (9): 601–603.
2. Conner, D.R. (1992). *Managing at the speed of change: How resilient managers succeed and prosper where others fail*. Villard.
3. Ibid.

Chapter 5

1. Most common frameworks were variations on Kotter's eight-step model (see discussion in Chapter 1) and the ADKAR model. ADKAR is a change model that describes the five outcomes needed for users to achieve successful change: creating awareness, desire, knowledge, ability to change, and reinforcement of the changes. ADKAR is often portrayed as a five-stage process. Hiatt, J. (2006). *ADKAR: A Model for Change in Business, Government, and our Community*. Prosci.
2. Ørsted, (2019). Making Green Energy Affordable-How the Offshore Wind Energy Industry Matured and What We Can Learn From It. Fredericia, Denmark. https://orsted.com/en/insights/white-papers/making-green-energy-affordable
3. Christensen, C.M., Hall, T., Dillon, K., and Duncan, D.S. (2016). Know your customers' jobs to be done. *Harvard Business Review* 94 (9): 54–62. https://hbr.org/2016/09/know-your-customers-jobs-to-be-done.

4. Strategyzer (n.d.) The value proposition canvas. https://www.strategyzer.com/library/the-value-proposition-canvas

5. Budzier, A., Blumberg, S., Gabrisch, N., et al. (2022). *The Secret to Unlocking Value in Tech Transformations: It's Not the Tech*. Whitepaper, Saïd Business School, University of Oxford.

6. Kotter, J.P. (1995). Leading change: Why transformation efforts fail. *Harvard Business Review*, May–June. https://hbr.org/1995/05/leading-change-why-transformation-efforts-fail-2&sa=D&source=docs&ust=1666601835036961&usg=AOvVaw1KIGcy7jgPaRnirWZLwdTz

7. Famously first codified in Royce, W.W. (August 1970). *Managing the Development of Large Software Systems: Concepts and Techniques. Proceedings, Technical Papers of Western Electronic Show and Convention*, 1–9. Institute of Electrical and Electronics Engineers.

8. In fact, early accounts of systems engineering approaches to large-scale software development projects suggest that the waterfall has always been an illusion and abstraction. Great examples of the gap between the mythical rational top-down process and what actually happened on the ground are the Sage and Atlas projects of the 1950s and 1960s, which are brilliantly documented in Hughes, T.P. (1998). *Rescuing Prometheus: Four Monumental Projects That Changed Our World*. Vintage.

9. Walker, S.K. (2005). *Capabilities-Based Planning-How It Is Intended to Work and Challenges to Its Successful Implementation*. Army War College.

10. However, the approach is not without challenges in project execution. The particular challenge lies in the capability or service integration. The shift from a command and control structure to leadership of expert teams to leadership of a system of teams is engagingly documented in McChrystal, G.S., Collins, T., Silverman, D., and Fussell, C. (2015). *Team of Teams: New Rules of Engagement for a Complex World*. Penguin.

11. Beer, M. and Nohria, N. (2000). Cracking the code of change. *Harvard Business Review* 78 (3): 133–141.

12. As part of the study, we tested 16 complexity factors that previous research identified to make the delivery of IT projects more difficult. Of the 16, we only found 2 complexity factors that were statistically significant for the transformation success: ineffective governance and high security requirements. We also tested 11 project management success factors. Of the 11, we only found 2 success factors that were statistically significant: effective risk management and stakeholder alignment. More detail is in Appendix.

13. Hubbard, D.W. (2014). *How to Measure Anything: Finding the Value of Intangibles in Business*. Wiley.

14. Ries, E. (2011). *The Lean Startup: How today's Entrepreneurs Use Continuous Innovation to Create Radically Successful Businesses*. Currency. Blank, S. (2013). Why the lean start-up changes everything. *Harvard Business Review* 91 (5): 63–72.
15. Obeng, E. (1994). *All Change: The Project Leader's Secret Handbook*. Financial Times-Prentice Hall.
16. Turner, R. and Cochrane, R. (1993). Goals-and-methods matrix: Coping with projects with ill-defined goals and methods of achieving them. *International Journal of Project Management* 11: 93–112.

Chapter 6

1. Tanik, M.M. and Yeh, R.T. (1989). *R*apid prototyping in software development. *Computer* 22 (5): 9–11.
2. Bowker, G.C. and Star, S.L. (2000). *Sorting Things Out: Classification and Its Consequences*. MIT Press.
3. Tulgan, B. (2020). Learn when to say no. . . and how to say yes. *Harvard Business Review* 98 (5): 135–139.
4. Kano, N. 1984, April. Attractive quality and must-be quality. *Hinshitsu: The Journal of the Japanese Society for Quality Control*, 14 (2): 39–48.
5. Lewrick, M., Link, P., and Leifer, L. (2018). *The Design Thinking Playbook: Mindful Digital Transformation of Teams, Products, Services, Businesses and Ecosystems*. John Wiley & Sons.

Chapter 7

1. Most of the organizations in our interviews had many more layers of hierarchy.
2. A key characteristic of all projects is their deadline. Projects have an expiry date right from the start – this makes them a temporary organization, an observation first described in Packendorff, J. (1995). Inquiring into the temporary organization: New directions for project management research. *Scandinavian Journal of Management* 11 (4): 319–333.
3. Lundin, R.A. and Söderholm, A. (1995). A theory of the temporary organization. Scandinavian Journal of Management 11 (4): 437–455.
4. The mean Support scores are statistically different in a pairwise comparison (all $p < 0.015$ with Holm adjustment). Promote and Own are not statistically significantly different in the pairwise comparisons.
5. For top and middle management, Support scores are all statistically significantly higher than Own and Promote scores (all $p < 0.02$, pairwise

comparison, Holm adjustment). There are no statistically significant differences between Support, Promote, and Own by frontline management.

6. Ganvik, K., Stise, R., Creasey, T. et al. (2020). *Best Practices in Change Management, 11th Edition. Prosci Benchmarking Report, 1863 Change Leaders Share Lessons and Best Practices in Change Management.* Prosci Research.

7. These questions are core to the empathy canvas from the book by Gray, D., Brown, S., and Macanufo, J. (2010). *Gamestorming: A Playbook for Innovators, Rulebreakers, and Changemakers.* O'Reilly Media A pdf version of the empathy canvas can be found at: https://gamestorming.com/.

8. A point made engagingly by Yves Morieux in his TED talks and his book: Morieux, Y. and Tollman, P. (2014). *Six Simple Rules: How to Manage Complexity Without Getting Complicated.* Harvard Business Review Press.

9. Police shot Brazilian eight times. (2005, July 25). *BBC News.* http://news.bbc.co.uk/2/hi/uk_news/4713753.stm.

Chapter 8

1. Hemp, P. (2009). Death by information overload. *Harvard Business Review* 87 (9): 82–89.

2. Barrett, D.J. (2002). Change communication: Using strategic employee communication to facilitate major change. *Corporate Communications: An International Journal* 7 (4): 219–231.

3. Smith, E.D. and Nyman, R.C. (1939). *Technology & Labor: A Study of the Human Problems of Labor Saving.* Institute of Human Relations.

4. Skinner, B.F. (1958). Reinforcement today. *American Psychologist* 13 (3): 94–99.

5. The more academic version is the result of a systematic literature review on behavioral theory in change published by Michie, S., Van Stralen, M.M., and West, R. (2011). The behaviour change wheel: A new method for characterising and designing behaviour change interventions. *Implementation Science* 6 (1): 1–12.

6. Heracleous, L., Wawarta, C., Paroutis, S., and Gonzalez, S. (2019). How a group of NASA renegades transformed mission control. *MIT Sloan Management Review* 5.

7. Fosfuri, A. and Rønde, T. (2009). Leveraging resistance to change and the skunk works model of innovation. *Journal of Economic Behavior & Organization* 72 (1): 274–289.

8. Celebrating success is, for example, Step 6 in Kotter's eight-step model of change, which we discussed in Chapter 1.

9. These projects followed the UK government guidelines for campaign planning called OASIS (Objectives, Audience insights, Strategy/Idea, Implementation, Scoring/Evaluation). More information is available at https://gcs.civilservice.gov.uk/guidance/marketing/delivering-government-campaigns/guide-to-campaign-planning-oasis.

10. Shibutani, T. (1966). *Improvised News*. Ardent Media.

11. Bowen, F., Newenham-Kahindi, A., and Herremans, I. (2010). When suits meet roots: the antecedents and consequences of community engagement strategy. *Journal of Business Ethics* 95 (2): 297–318.

12. Sinek, S. (2009). *Start with Why: How Great Leaders Inspire Everyone to Take Action*. Penguin Publishing Group.

13. Implement Consulting Group (ed.). (November 2022). *Change Communication X-ray 2022: A health check on organizational change communication*. https://implementconsultinggroup.com/article/change-communication-x-ray-2022.

Chapter 9

1. Graesser, A.C., Sabatini, J.P., and Li, H. (2022). Educational psychology is evolving to accommodate technology, multiple disciplines, and twenty-first-century skills. *Annual Review of Psychology* 73: 547–574.

2. Ibid.

3. Graesser, A.C., Sabatini, J.P., and Li, H. (2022). Educational psychology is evolving to accommodate technology, multiple disciplines, and twenty-first-century skills. *Annual Review of Psychology* 73 (1): 547–574.

4. Brysbaert, M. (2019). How many words do we read per minute? A review and meta-analysis of reading rate. *Journal of Memory and Language* 109: https://doi.org/10.1016/j.jml.2019.104047.

5. Tools for Clear Speech, Baruch College. (2024). Speaking rate. (n.d.). https://tfcs.baruch.cuny.edu/speaking-rate

6. Davachi, L., Kiefer, T., Rock, D., and Rock, L. (2010). Learning that lasts through AGES. *NeuroLeadership Journal* 3: 53–63.

7. Ibid.

Chapter 10

1. Carmeli, A., Brueller, D., and Dutton, J.E. (2009). Learning behaviours in the workplace: the role of high-quality interpersonal relationships and psychological safety. *Systems Research and Behavioral Science: The*

Official Journal of the International Federation for Systems Research 26 (1): 81–98.

Edmondson, A.C. and Lei, Z. (2014). Psychological safety: the history, renaissance, and future of an interpersonal construct. *Annual Review of Organizational Psychology and Organizational Behavior* 1 (1): 23–43.

Bond-Barnard, T.J., Fletcher, L., and Steyn, H. (2018). Linking trust and collaboration in project teams to project management success. *International Journal of Managing Projects in Business* 11 (2): 432–457.

2. Brown, S.P. and Leigh, T.W. (1996). A new look at psychological climate and its relationship to job involvement, effort, and performance. *Journal of Applied Psychology* 81 (4): 358.

3. Self-expression means that "no one want to put on a 'work face' when they go to an office"; we want to know that work is more than just a job (Charles Duhigg, "What Google Learned from Its Quest to Build the Perfect Team," *New York Times*, February 2, 2016).

4. Sauer, C. (1993). *Why Information Systems Fail: A Case Study Approach (Information Systems)*. Alfred Waller.

5. Gefen, D. (2004). What makes an ERP implementation relationship worthwhile: linking trust mechanisms and ERP usefulness. *Journal of Management Information Systems* 21 (1): 263–288.

6. For an up-to-date review of the role of trust in project management, see: Cerić, A., Vukomanović, M., Ivić, I., and Kolarić, S. (2021). Trust in megaprojects: a comprehensive literature review of research trends. *International Journal of Project Management* 39 (4): 325–338.

7. Gefen, *What makes an ERP implementation relationship worthwhile*.

8. Schaupp, L.C. and Carter, L. (2010). The impact of trust, risk and optimism bias on E-file adoption. *Information Systems Frontiers* 12 (3): 299–309.

Tung, F.C., Chang, S.C., and Chou, C.M. (2008). An extension of trust and TAM model with IDT in the adoption of the electronic logistics information system in HIS in the medical industry. *International Journal of Medical Informatics* 77 (5): 324–335.

9. Cerić, A., et al., *Trust in megaprojects*.

10. Chawla, A. and Kelloway, E.K. (2004). Predicting openness and commitment to change. *Leadership and Organization Development Journal* 25: 485–498.

11. Maister, D.H., Galford, R., and Green, C. (2000). *The Trusted Advisor*. Free Press.

12. Goldsmith, M. and Morgan, H. (2004). Leadership is a contact sport: the 'follow-up factor' in management development. *Strategy + Business* 36: https://www.strategy-business.com/article/04307.

Appendix B

1. A further possible grouping by activity across levels of management does not converge due to the high correlation within each level of management.
2. Maylor, H., Vidgen, R., and Carver, S. (2008). Managerial complexity in project-based operations: a grounded model and its implications for practice. *Project Management Journal* 39 (1_suppl): S15–S26.
3. Jones, C. (1999). Software sizing. *IEE Review* 45 (4): 165–167.
4. Flyvbjerg, B. (2006). From Nobel prize to project management: getting risks right. *Project Management Journal* 37 (3): 5–15.
5. Fortune, J. and White, D. (2006). Framing of project critical success factors by a systems model. *International Journal of Project Management* 24 (1): 53–65.

About the Authors

Dr Alexander Budzier

Dr Alexander Budzier is a Fellow at the University of Oxford's Saïd Business School.

He is part of Oxford's research group on major programs. His particular focus is on comparing sectors. He has studied projects and programs in IT, infrastructure, energy, defense, mega-events, and other industries. In 2015, Alexander was named a Fellow in Management Practice.

Alexander is the academic director of several Major Projects Leadership Academies, and he designs and directs corporate education programs. He regularly teaches at Oxford's MSc for Major Programme Management, the MBA program, and the UK Major Projects Leadership Academy.

Before joining Oxford University, Alexander worked at T-Mobile International as a consultant with McKinsey's Business Technology Office in Düsseldorf and Chicago. He then co-founded Oxford Global Projects, a specialist consultancy where he applies insights, data, and world-leading research to real-life projects.

Thomas Gottschalck

Thomas Gottschalck is a senior partner at Implement Consulting Group. Thomas heads Implement's digital and transformation services related to the public sector. Thomas has more than 15 years of experience with large-scale IT transformation and program management across industries, with a dedicated focus on organizational adjustments related to digital change initiatives.

Thomas is the director of Implement's experience-based customer networks for project and program managers. In addition to this role, he spearheads other strategic industry research and partnership initiatives to promote continuous development and improve the success rate of digital transformation projects.

Kim Bjørn Thuesen

Kim is a partner and head of the IT Change Management department at Implement Consulting Group.

Kim has more than 15 years of practical experience managing change in large IT implementations in global organizations. He is an expert on empowering middle managers to be in front of change, inventing engaging training setups, and deploying effective communication, thereby ensuring that the organizations he helps realize the full benefits of their IT investments.

For the last seven years, Kim and Dr. Alexander Budzier have been researching change management's impact on the success of IT projects.

Astrid Lanng

Astrid Lanng is an experienced management consultant from Implement Consulting Group, where she is part of the Digital Transformation practice. She focuses on helping large-scale IT programs succeed by achieving business benefits and delivering on time and budget.

Astrid has almost ten years of experience in project and change management. Astrid has unique expertise in driving projects forward, ensuring key stakeholders are involved, and providing input. Furthermore, Astrid has ample experience designing and delivering engaging large-scale training programs and facilitating impactful workshops.

In addition to her practical experience, Astrid has been a core part of the research project, which has delivered the foundation for this book.

Index

Page numbers followed by *f* and *t* refer to figures and tables, respectively.